Lirda Fravek (handwritten signature)

"Whether you are seeking the meaning of your soul's journey or are searching for clear next steps in your journey, search no further. Combining biblical stories, deep intellect, and above all, a rich soul, Marjory Bankson has created a companion and deeply insightful roadmap that can help us make meaning out of our experiences."

—Michael F. Murray, President,
Creative Interchange Consultants

"For exploring call, Marjory Bankson's *The Call to the Soul* is simply the best resource available. Marjory provides guidelines for a journey of discovery and transformation."

—The Rev. Dick Busch, Center for Continuing
Education, Virginia Theological Seminary

"Marjory Bankson is a skilled writer, teacher, and spiritual guide. She supports her carefully laid out pattern of spiritual development with biblical scholarship, knowledge of Jungian psychology, her own experience and that of many others, as well as her extensive reading of the spiritual giants of many faiths."

—Rev. Dr. Florence W. Pert, Founder, Executive
Director of SpiritWorks, Marble Collegiate
Church, New York City

D1367317

•

ALSO BY MARJORY ZOET BANKSON

This Is My Body: Creativity, Clay, and Change

Braided Streams: Esther and a Woman's Way of Growing

Seasons of Friendship: Naomi & Ruth as a Pattern

•

The Call to the Soul

Six Stages of
Spiritual Development

by Marjory Zoet Bankson

Augsburg Books

THE CALL TO THE SOUL
Six Stages of Spiritual Development

First Augsburg Books edition © 2005. Copyright © 1999 Marjory Zoet Bankson
International Copyright secured. All rights reserved. Printed and bound in the United
States.

Large-quantity purchases or custom editions of this book are available at a discount
from the publisher. For more information, contact the sales department at Augsburg
Fortress, Publishers, 1-800-328-4648, or write to: Sales Director, Augsburg Fortress
Publishers, P. O. Box 1209, Minneapolis, MN 55440-1209.

ISBN 0-8066-9035-6

Cover design and illustrations by Hugh Duffy. Cover image by Sara Steele. Detail from
"The Forces of Attraction" copyright © 1984, 1988 by Sara Steele. All rights reserved.

Quotations from the biblical story of Gideon are from the New Revised Standard Version
of the Bible, copyright © 1946, 1952, 1971, 1989 by the Division of Christian Education of
the National Council of the Churches of Christ in the USA. Used by permission.

Quotations from the biblical story of Esther are from The Jerusalem Bible, copyright ©
1966 by Darton, Longman, & Todd, Ltd. and Doubleday, a division of Random House, Inc.
Reprinted by permission.

PUBLISHER'S NOTE: Permission is graciously extended by the author for study groups
using The Call to the Soul to reproduce "The Cycle of Call" diagram on page 39.

The paper used in this publication meets the minimum requirements of American
National Standard for Information Sciences—Permanence of Paper for Printed Library
Materials, ANSI Z329.48-1984. ♾™

Manufactured in the U.S.A.

09   08   07   06   05   1   2   3   4   5   6   7   8   9   10

•

*For Marianne Johnson and Michael Vermillion
who called me to my work in the world.*

•

•

. . . no matter what the stage or grade of life,
the call rings up the curtain, always,
on a mystery of transfiguration . . .
which, when complete,
amounts to a dying and a birth.
—Joseph Campbell

•

• *The Call to the Soul* •

Contents

Acknowledgments

Without the pioneering vision of Gordon and Mary Cosby, founders of The Church of the Saviour in Washington, D.C., in 1947, none of this would have been possible. They cultivated a new generation of leadership and have blessed the birth of a dozen small congregations since 1976. Without the passionate books by Elizabeth O'Connor, I would not have known about The Church of the Saviour. Her bibliographies provided my earliest theological education, and her descriptions of the journey inward/journey outward quickened my call to a deeper life.

Living from a sense of call is the core concept at The Seekers Church, one of the six small churches formed around mission groups at The Church of the Saviour in 1976. My husband, Peter, and I arrived just one month after these sister communities began, and we chose Seekers because of its commitment to shared leadership and because most Seekers are involved in some form of child advocacy. It has been a place to share creativity, care, and commitment, particularly with the others in my mission group: Ron Arms, Ken Burton, Anne Beaufort, David Lloyd, Dan Phillips, Margreta Silverstone, and Carolyn Shields. I am indebted to Seekers for many of the ideas, observations, and conversations included in this book, and to Sonya Dyer for nurturing the vision of Seekers so faithfully from the beginning.

I am also indebted to the Board of Faith At Work, particularly the women who mentored me in developing the basic retreat design described in the Appendix, which we have used since 1980: Nancy Boyle, Florence Pert, Maggie Everett, and Pat Minard.

They taught me the power of relational and experiential Bible study and helped develop the Women's Ministry of Faith At Work, where most of these concepts were tested. Since Faith At Work began with the ministry of Sam Shoemaker at Calvary Episcopal Church in New York City in 1927, it has provided a relational and ecumenical understanding of spiritual growth in community through its magazine, *Faith@Work,* and its retreat ministry. Since I became president in 1985, Faith At Work has been my call and my vocation.

In 1992, when we moved the Faith At Work office to Falls Church, Virginia, I shared office space with two creative women who were using their own process for organizational analysis known as "The Change Cycle." As Interchange International, Lillie Brock and Mary Ann Salerno work with personal and organizational change in the business world. They encouraged me to publish this book as a way for people to explore the spiritual dimension of their "Change Cycle." I have used their visual format for the soulwork cycle and thank them for their generosity, their input, and their encouragement.

The Call to the Soul would also not have been possible without the love, support, and tolerance of my husband, Peter, who has shared my sense of commitment to our marriage as a crucible for spiritual growth.

And finally, I am grateful for the encouragement and guidance of my editor and friend, Marcia Broucek of Innisfree Press. Her commitment to offering classic books for spiritual growth speaks of her own call to the "deep heart's core" where we are truly fed.

Introduction

Most people think of "call" or "calling" in a vocational sense, as in "What is the special thing I am supposed to be doing?" Many associate call with a full-time religious vocation—primarily for clergy and missionaries. But today, interest in spirituality and call has spilled out of churches into everyday life.

There was a time when call was the exclusive province of the church. Only people who felt "called" into a monastery or full-time ministry were seen as living a "spiritual" life, and everyone else simply went about their daily work, letting those who felt "called" lead them in rituals of worship. There was little in between the two lifestyles. This tradition of separating faith from daily work was intentionally promoted by the American constitutional separation of church and state. It was unintentionally promoted by setting Sunday aside as a day for worship, designating only certain buildings for spiritual activity and recognizing only specific people as spiritual leaders. Until the early sixties, "Blue Laws" kept stores closed and churches open on Sunday.

In the past forty years, the influence of traditional religion has decreased markedly, yet at the same time, ordinary people are awakening to the importance of Spirit in daily life and work. In fact, if you are reading this book, you are already considering the personal dimensions of your spiritual life. Your questions indicate your engagement in the search for understanding your call, your reason for being. Your critical thought process is a measure of your discernment. Your caution, a measure of respect for the size and meaning of call.

I see "call" not as a vocational choice but as a special way of understanding of what we are here for: being able to name our changing field of work in the world and to know when it is complete, when it is time for a new call to begin. When we live out a call to write or teach or build or parent in such a way that we treat life as a sacred gift, we are responding to an invitation to wholeness. We are also responding to the unseen mystery and holiness of life itself.

After twenty years of working in the field of soul development through the magazine and retreat ministry of Faith At Work, I have seen hundreds of people wake up to the notion that there is a purpose for their lives, a work to complete, some task or creation or contribution they are called to in the present time. Some go to a church or a retreat center to discover their calling; others agonize alone or search out the support of a community to help discern the path. In reality, most of us do not have a place where call is honored, where a new call can be birthed. We are left with the individual burden of hearing and interpreting the whispers of God's call without the help of a community for discernment and direction, so we come like cautious animals, sniffing the air and testing the ground.

My first experience of call began in a mortuary and ended in a pastor's office, some eight months later. As a young teen, I had begun practicing the pipe organ in a local mortuary because the church was cold during the week and the mortuary was warm. The room where I practiced was always dark when I entered except for a small light that illuminated any casket that shared my space. Often the lid was open, in preparation for a viewing that day. I always checked to see who was there, laid out so carefully and stiffly. I was shocked by the children, awed by the difference in faces and dress, stunned when I realized it could easily be one of my sisters, or me.

I wondered especially about the young ones. Why had they died so soon? What purpose had their short lives accomplished? Even then I discarded the notion that death was a punishment for bad behavior, reckoning that a three-year-old had not had time to do anything bad enough to die for. Instead, death called me into the presence of life's mysterious source, and I began to feel something stirring in me, to grasp some concept of the gift of life. I began to feel that my life might have a purpose beyond what I was conscious of.

My questions began to connect with the language of the church, where the pastor referred to great biblical figures as (mostly) men who had been "called" by God to do something heroic, something beyond what they imagined for themselves. We learned about little David who killed Goliath, and other heroes of the faith, such as Abraham, Joseph, and Moses, who overcame insurmountable odds with God's intervention and help. "Call" seemed to imply that God would be available with miraculous assistance. Even Jonah's story of spending a time of repentance in the belly of a whale underscored God's assistance when someone finally said "yes" to God's direction.

Although in my church, the notion of "call" was reserved for those who might enter "full-time Christian service," I began to feel that God might be speaking to me in a language I did not yet understand, so I went to see our minister, saying that I thought I was being called to the mission field. (While there were no official places of leadership for women in the American church at that time, the church did send women to serve overseas!). The pastor listened politely, then smiled and said, "Well, I think your hormones will catch up with you soon enough."

Somewhat bewildered by his answer, I left, knowing my sense of call had been dismissed by a professional man of God. I assumed he was right and I was wrong. I tucked away my intuition of call and turned my face in the direction of government service instead, not even aware of the possibility that "call" might take form in the "secular" realm.

Now I know that call is not confined to the church. Any field can be the place where we find meaning and purpose in our work, whether paid or unpaid. Call engages our feelings and intellect toward some larger end, toward some greater goal than that which we can accomplish alone.

Over time, I have seen a certain pattern to the way people come to recognize and claim their call. I have also seen how one call can be completed and another welcomed. Now I know there is no perfect job or vocation, no single call that fits our gifts like no other, but rather an invitation to partnership with God in a larger work of learning that we are all interconnected, that we are all part of God's living being. That means there will be several specific calls in a lifetime.

Almost every other aspect of our living and dying has been categorized into stages: pregnancy, the first years of life, mid-life passages, death and dying. But our spiritual development remains essentially uncharted. *The Call to the Soul* offers a spiritual road-map, a six-stage soulwork cycle that I have come to understand as a natural and consistent process.

Knowing that there is a pattern and progression to call can be encouraging when we feel lost and alone with impulses we do not understand. Becoming conscious of the way call weaves between the individual and community can be a guide to what we need to do next. Although I believe we can enter the cycle at any point, my experience has been that the stages of call unfold in the pattern I am presenting—as a spiral journey with inward and outward dimensions. Over time, we will experience not one, but several calls. Knowing where we are in each cycle can offer comfort, companionship, and guidance in an otherwise lonely journey. I also believe that understanding the process of call can freshen our conversations about meaning and purpose, provide guidance for people who want to believe in God, and encourage the formation of informal spiritual communities.

My hope is that you will read this book with others and share your reflections together. I have included some of my own stories to stimulate your thoughts and written response. Each stage raises some obvious questions, some of which are noted in the Appendix "A Soulwork Cycle Retreat." While the retreat design is based on using the material for a weekend event, I have included suggestions for a format that could be covered in one day. Consider, also, sharing your responses aloud with a partner or small group on a weekly basis, one stage at a time, as you explore your sense of call.

The Nature Of Call

CHAPTER 1

In my dream, I am in a crowded airport, shuffling papers aimlessly. Suddenly I hear my name paged. As I approach the desk, I see a long line of people, waiting to be checked in. When I tell the agent my name and that I've been paged, she looks alarmed and motions me to enter the dark tunnel behind her, saying "Hurry, your plane is leaving. Maybe you can make it." I enter the tunnel and notice a limp figure slumped over a ticket counter, but I do not stop.

S oulwork begins when something breaks through the smug shell of self-reliance that our culture calls "success." Most often it is pain and anguish because nothing else is strong enough to crack the ego defenses that we build to cope with our existential anxiety. Sometimes the signal comes with illness or disturbing dreams. The Spirit rises inside, and yet we are not ready to let go of the old way. Even if it is difficult, at least it is familiar.

In the dream I describe above, I am "shuffling papers," apparently bored and waiting for my high-flying organizational plane/ego to be called. Instead, I am called by name over the loudspeaker. The call is specific, urgent, and separates me from the crowd. The level of anxiety is high both for me and for the agent at the desk. She wishes me well but cannot help me directly. I must proceed on foot with no guarantee of success. Metaphorically, the dream describes how a call comes.

Sometimes we have been comfortable enough so that the cry of open need does not happen until external security is stripped away by a move, a job loss, or the illness of a loved one. As Sam Shoemaker, founder of Faith At Work, once wrote, "Every spiritual journey begins with two words: Help! Help!"[1] A cry for help reverberates with hope that we are not alone, that someone or some thing can and will respond. Whether we call that "otherness" God or Spirit, the I-Thou relationship or Ground of Being, we want to know that we are part of some larger reality when we come to the end of our ego solutions. Most of us are not open to call until we come to the point of crying "Help! Help!"

Even when our conscious minds reject interdependence as "childish," something in us knows that we are connected to a web of life that we cannot count or control. Mystics point the way with poetry and paint. Artists give us visual symbols to link *chronos* and *kairos* worlds of time and eternity. Myth-makers tell the tale in metaphoric form. Our dreams suggest a realm not far removed that is full of wisdom for the way we are to go. And biblical stories provide us with a vision of who the Caller is—what the nature of God is—and the kinds of work to which we might be called. As we dialogue with this unknown Source, something new is brought into being through us. Soulwork is the essence of that creative dialogue, and the soulwork cycle a pattern of call that resonates through human history.

• *INVITATION* •

Once I thought that by looking at what I loved to do, what my skills and gifts were, I would know what I was "supposed" to be doing with my time and energy. Thinking that my "calling" was primarily a vocational choice, I learned to ask questions about my vision for the world in which I live, then add my values and information about my personality type, along with some input on my style of leadership and ways of handling conflict.

But in the last years of my father's life, I found myself thinking about call differently. As he struggled to live as fully as he could with a diminishing range of mobility due to bone cancer, I found myself asking what was his call *then?* Beyond the workplace. Beyond being productive. I began to realize that call was bigger than work, deeper than one's contribution to society. My dad taught me about the call to meaning and purpose even beyond our last breath. In a sense, his call is still alive in the words I am writing.

Now I would say that call is an invitation to wholeness, a spiritual prompting to complete the work of love that we are here to do. Call is "built in" to our physical and psychic makeup, and it takes form as we interact with the world around us. It comes neither from inside or out, but is a product of both.

The concept of call assumes we are spiritually linked with others and with creation, whether we like it or not. Even though psychologists speak of "autonomy" as an essential stage of development, and our culture values individualism and self-reliance above other human values, call suggests that autonomy is an aspect of *relationship* rather than a lasting state of individualism. We separate in order to recognize that we are related—not only to each other but to God.

Attending to call implies belief in a Greater Being and the possibility of making connection with the unseen realm of Spirit that holds all things together. Attending to call implies that we can have that connection at the same time we are conscious of our mortality and the physical limits of living in time. Mystics have sought that connection through prayer and meditation; artists, through their creativity; and religious communities, through their common life and worship. The earth, with its cycles of seasons, speaks to our souls of a larger story in which we each have a part, but we must quiet the incessant voices of rational problem-solving to hear the heartbeat of creation in our veins.

• *BODY SENSE* •

Call begins with a feeling of connection to someone or something, a synapse of the soul. When we walk by the ocean, watch a changing sunset, or hold a newborn child, we often feel that we belong to something larger. When we craft something with our hands, we slow down to a rhythm and quality of attention that helps us notice the way newness is born through our hands or the way a particular piece fits with a larger design. Sometimes call comes as a feeling of anger at injustice: *"It shouldn't have to be this way!"* A sensual experience of wonder or longing—or even deep weariness—is often another clue to call.

Attending to call requires space and time for listening—time between hurried appointments, unopened mail, and procrastinated phone calls. It is not a matter of sitting still to listen so much as it is getting in touch with the perceptiveness of body, of sensibilities and intuitions, dreams and coincidences, for noticing the ways we belong to a larger reality.

Our physical bodies belong to the realm of linear, or *chronos,* time. Life in *chronos* time is a matter of getting through one thing after another, a never-ending series of hurdles that mark a path from birth to death. But the timeless realm of God is *kairos* time. Gordon Cosby at The Church of the Saviour in Washington, D.C. speaks of call as that which connects daily life in *chronos* time with *kairos* or eternity.[2] It is the essential crossing point between God and human life. For too long we have assumed it was the job of professional clergy to tend that crossing point when, in fact, call is the province of everyone capable of consciousness.

When our response to call takes us beyond ourselves, beyond convenience and entitlement, beyond self-esteem and sobriety to a larger purpose that has to do with what we understand as God's intention for all of creation, then we embark on a lifelong journey of revelation and adventure. When we begin to hear God's call, we leave the isolation of own independence and autonomy for something more challenging and fulfilling: the invitation to be a conscious part of the cosmic dance of creation.

Maybe it is the "bigness" of call that frightens us away from this sense of mystical connection. Instead, we concentrate on the "small stuff"—such as what to do and where to go, planning and scheduling, so we have virtually no time left for larger visions. We segment our lives into spiritual and physical, as the Greeks before us did, and we take the practical path, concentrating on "getting the job done." While huge numbers of Americans tell the pollsters that they "believe in God" and "pray regularly," most keep their faith in a spiritual dimension entirely separate from daily life and work. Like the ancient gnostics, we separate body from spirit. Attending to call means accepting the possibility of spiritual guidance and integration with a more comprehensive worldview.

• *SOULWORK* •

I make a distinction between soul and spirit because it speaks to the difference between Greek dualism, which separates body and spirit, and Hebrew integration, which wraps the two into one as "soul." Call belongs to the earthy realm of soul where body and spirit intertwine. One gift of the Black church, and its cultural counterpart in blues music, has been the expression of "soul" where body and spirit "get down" together. Soul music sings of hardship and hope, gutsy women and lonely men. The soulwork of call begins here, at the core of the human heart. Soulwork is common, ordinary and fleshy, acquainted with grief and heartache, as well as pleasure and peace.

Often it takes pain to wake us up, to remind us why we are alive, to call forth soul. The challenge of overcoming barriers may demand resources we did not know were there. We may discover depths only dimly suspected. A woman from Iowa who was widowed in a farm accident once told me that she gardens to tend her soul "because it reminds me that I belong to forever." That is the doorway to call: recognizing the possibility that we can receive guidance from the unseen realm of Spirit even as we crumble clods of dirt with our fingers.

• *TRANSITION* •

Some years ago, William Bridges described a three-stage process of endings, neutrality, and beginnings for dealing with soulwork in organizations—even though he did not use the term "soulwork." He differentiated internal transition from external change. While change happens *to* us, he said, transition is an *internal process* that begins with closure and grief, proceeds through a neutral zone, and finally comes to a new beginning. Bridges used the biblical story of Moses to teach this three-part cycle to business leaders. In the first period, Bridges said, Moses denied the call to lead his people out of Egypt, toward freedom. Then Bridges described an interim stage full of hesitation and vacillation as the "plague period" when nothing went right for Pharaoh or the Israelites. Only when we have completed the first two stages, concluded Bridges, can we really forge a new identity from the inside out.[3]

As Bridges demonstrated with his work on internal transitions for organizations, the biblical understanding of call is singularly free of church dogma. Throughout the Bible, God calls people to action, to new roles and responsibilities on behalf of others. As I worked with these biblical stories of call, I realized that Bridges' three-part framework was a general pattern with broader application. As my own understanding of call became more conscious, I began choosing a biblical story as the backbone of each Faith At Work retreat I led because I found it gave people a way to continue their inner work beyond the time we spent together: They could always go back to the biblical story and be reminded of the process of call. At a recent workshop, people asked to choose a favorite biblical story of "call" came up with this list:

- ABRAHAM—called to leave his homeland without knowing where God would lead.
- SARAH—called to bear a child when she had given up hope.
- HAGAR—called to trust God's promise that her child would thrive.
- JACOB—called to reconcile with his brother, Esau.
- SAMUEL—called beyond his mentor, Eli, to hear God's voice directly.
- THE DISCIPLES—called away from their fishing nets to follow Jesus.
- MARY AND MARTHA—called to believe in resurrection when their brother, Lazarus, was brought back from the dead.
- MARY MAGDALENE—called to "go and tell" what she had seen of the risen Christ to disbelieving disciples.
- PETER—called to "feed my sheep" after denying that he knew Jesus.
- SAUL—called to a new name and a new work on the road to Damascus.
- LYDIA—called to found a church with Paul's tutelage in Philippi.

Over a twenty-year period, as I have studied these stories and listened to people wrestle with the question of call, I have recognized a six-stage cycle of call with a definite crossing point in the middle.

Initially, call comes with an explosion of possibility—a burst of newness and radical change that breaks into the *chronos* realm of everyday time. Then the first two stages of human response are usually conservative, full of hesitation, suspicion, and fear as we question the reality of the call itself. At first, we *RESIST* (Stage One) the call to new life, and then we begin to *RECLAIM* (Stage Two) forgotten or rejected parts of our story in the light of a new call—even as we deny or resist it.

Then a middle or neutral phase starts with a clear *REVELA-TION* (Stage Three) of what we might do and how we might do it. That vision creates tension between what we have been doing and a call to a new way of being. If the call is strong enough and our response deep enough, we come to a crossing point that requires a definite decision to embody the call publicly and relate to others through our call.

We do have the power to refuse call—that is our human freedom. We can stay on the side of dreaming and possibility without crossing into embodiment. We can hesitate and turn back, repeating the first three stages in an endless waltz of agitation. Or we can cross what I call the *"POISON RIVER"* and choose to trust the call that has been beckoning. The name "Poison River" comes from a childhood game, but the concept of crossing a river barrier is ancient and archetypal.

The last three stages of the soulwork cycle are not free of fear and doubt, but once across the "Poison River," it is much easier to complete the cycle, moving through *RISK* (Stage Four), where we make our call visible to others, to Stage Five, where we *RELATE* to a wider community who can share in our sense of purpose. Finally, we *RELEASE* (Stage Six) power, prestige, and control to make space for starting a new cycle all over again.

• *JUST ONE CALL?* •

Traditionally, men have achieved identity through their work, and that has shaped our understanding of call. Until recently, a man's work was usually one career path, one job, or moving up in one company. People who changed jobs were suspect, judged unstable or unreliable. As a result, our notion of call has been a singular and specific work or vocational direction. The biblical understanding of call has contributed to that limited notion because the Bible is full of heroic individuals who were called by God to a specific task, as though call were reserved for special people in special circumstances. Unfortunately, that heroic image has shaded call with savior overtones and put it out of reach for most.

But if call has to do with discovering our particular field of action or the part of God's realm that is ours to tend at any given time, then we must broaden those categories and consider whether we might find purpose in caring for our family at one stage and the freedom to use our gifts for painting or business or political organization at another stage.

The experiences of women are helpful here. At one time, a woman's life was identified by her body changes, and her work was primarily to bear children. Nobody spoke of women being "called" to that function, it was simply assumed. Women were automatically seen in one of three stages: Virgin, Mother, or Crone. Death came early and often to women in childbirth, and public life was left to men. Now, however, the average life expectancy for women is eighty years. Does that mean women go directly from childcaring to Crone? When I moved into menopause, I did not feel like a wise old crone; in fact, I was just beginning to enter a more public sphere as president of Faith At Work. I now identify this phase as being Woman in the world. Taking her place between the stages of Mother and Crone, being Woman suggests a four-cycle pattern: Virgin, Mother, Woman, and Crone.

From that departure, I began to wonder if there might be a different call in each stage of life. In my years of working among people seeking guidance about call, I have seen a clear relationship between what developmental psychologists identify as the major tasks for adult life and what I believe is the essence of call at each stage.

- In the first round or cycle of adult life, from age twenty to thirty-five, call seems to center around the question of identity: *"WHO AM I?"* It is also a time when we separate from our biological family and seek a separate identity through financial self-sufficiency and/or marriage.

- From thirty-five to fifty, most of us focus on finding our vocational call and achieving some financial stability. Moving beyond the simple question of a job, the question becomes *"WHAT IS MY WORK?"* Our search for work that contributes to a greater good means claiming a wider context and perhaps naming it as call.

- From fifty to sixty-five, we begin to grapple with the reality of death and physical limits and move beyond ego development to the question of *"WHAT IS MY GIFT?"* The question of "my gift" implies a sense of gratitude and identification with others who can celebrate our creativity with us.

- The last stage, from sixty-five to eighty and beyond, grows out of an acceptance of death and an embrace of God's timeless story of creation. That call becomes *"WHAT IS MY LEGACY?"* Seeing diminishment and death as limits on life's unquenchable desire for being gives the final round special urgency, even adventure. When we understand that call outlasts the marketplace and gives us a sense of meaning and value beyond producing income, then attending to call moves us beyond questions of career satisfaction into the realm of spiritual completion.

Who Am I?

What Is My Work?

What Is My Gift?

What Is My Legacy?

• *DEMOGRAPHIC GROUPINGS* •

One of the factors that makes the question of sequential calls so relevant is the dramatic segmentation by age and experience in our society. Never before in history has society been so differentiated by the technological and social conditions that shape childhood and early adulthood. Today there are four major age groups in the adult population, each making an impact on public policy and common resources, each ready for a distinct kind of call. In each grouping, age and circumstances affect call differently. While the concept of call as a single, lifelong vocation does not mean much to any of these four age-groups today, the biblical understanding of call as a quickening of one's relationship with God is something that all four age groups are seeking, each in their own way.

Builders, born before 1929

Born prior to the Stock Market Crash, Builders grew up during the Depression, went to college on the GI Bill after World War II, and came of age in the euphoric postwar period. Builders established suburban communities because cars made commuting possible, and they created the largest generation of babies in American history (the so-called Baby Boomers, born between 1946 and 1964). They "saved the world for democracy" and wanted to enjoy the fruits of that victory. They built homes, churches, schools, and manufacturing plants outside of urban centers, depending on cheap gas to link the parts of society. They believed in America, fought Communism in Korea and the Cold War in the fifties, struggled with social change in the sixties, and generally supported extension of the New Deal in President Johnson's social welfare legislation. Builders still tend to trust institutions and to look for strong caring leaders. Commitment is a strong value for Builders who were willing to give their lives for what they believed in.

Men and women of the Builder generation understood commitment so well that they gave their lives to institutions now run by younger people who do not seem to appreciate the sacrifice. One Builder remarked to me, "That's my blood all over the floor at the church. I gave it my all, and they hardly said thanks when I retired from the staff. I can't stand to go there now." Since the social unrest of the sixties, Builders have lived with criticism from their Boomer children. Many Builders question whether the legacy of their life experience can be received by younger generations—though there is no doubt about their eagerness for monetary inheritance.

Now past seventy, Builders are living longer, healthier lives than their parents did. Builders who outlive their contemporaries must form new relationships as old friends die or they move to be closer to their children. While many Builders are still active in the churches that served as a center for social life when their Baby-Boomer children were growing up, others are struggling to build community in new places without the relational skills for creating self-governing small groups.

Call for this age group revolves around relationships, tending old ones and finding new ones with people who are walking the path toward conscious aging and, ultimately, toward death. As questions of health and mobility remind them of their mortality, the soulwork cycle for Builders can be a time for integration and generosity instead of fearful clinging to privacy and property without a sense of call. Their primary question is, *"What is my legacy?"*

Bridgers, born 1929 - 1945

Born in the Depression and World War II years, Bridgers form a numerically small generation between the Builders and Boomers. They reached early adulthood in the fifties and sixties, understood hardship and commitment because of the war, generally married right out of college, and had their kids early before "the pill" was widely available. Most were not directly involved in the civil rights or anti-Vietnam protests of the sixties, but many experienced marital stress as the Feminist Movement of the seventies began to open doors for women in public life. In the eighties, Bridger women went to work in droves after their children were grown.

Bridgers tend to be very loyal, though they are more likely than Builders to look critically at unlimited commitments. In the classes I teach at Virginia Theological Seminary, pastors report that Bridgers often will work long and hard to sustain the very institutions that Boomers are willing to jettison. Bridgers may be the last age group with strong roots in the church, loyalty to denominations, and general knowledge of the Bible from long years in Sunday School. Many are providing the energy and leadership to keep smaller churches alive, but they are getting tired and often hope to retire earlier than their parents did.

For Bridgers, call usually means finding time for reflection, deepening relationships, and volunteer or part-time work after retirement. Many are looking forward to spending more time alone or with their adult children, who seem to have more trouble establishing independent homes for themselves. When to leave main-stream employment and focus on another kind of work is the question for many Bridgers today, as many are being pushed aside by aggressive Boomer reorganizations and buyouts. Finding a basis for self-worth beyond work is the primary spiritual task for Bridgers. Their question of call is, *"What is my gift?"*

Boomers, born 1946 - 1964

Boomers form the largest generation in American history. They began to come of age just after President Kennedy was assassinated in 1963. They rebelled against the Ozzie-and-Harriet world of their parents with drugs, sexual freedom for women on "the pill," and anti-Vietnam protests. Their world was shaped by TV, the Beatles, and tribal gatherings such as Woodstock. As adults, their work world was revolutionized by personal computers, entrepreneurial economics, and the driven schedules of two-career families. Children came later for Boomers as the biological clock ticked on toward forty. Divorce and drug-use, greed and violence at home have marred the material success of many.

Because the Boomer generation is so large, their needs have impacted social institutions from the time they started school. Many come to middle-age without the grounding of community and church-related traditions that provide the myths and meaning for times of vulnerability. Today, Boomers are creating new institutions and social policies to fit the lifestyle of two-career families. The mega-church movement caters to this Woodstock generation, providing the size and program variety that many Boomers expect from the consumer society in which they grew up. They want professional leadership, consumer sensitivity, and quick results.

Time is the most precious commodity for Boomers, and they pack as much into their busy schedules as possible, reserving time for self-care as earlier generations did not. Time pressures make long-term commitments seem impossible for Boomers, and they have changed the working environment for everyone with their faith in quick-response, just-in-time organizational mobility.

Boomers are concerned primarily with matters of work and family, ego accomplishment, and assertion of their power into the world. Although they are now trying to launch their children and influence public policy to sustain the material prosperity that they have enjoyed, moving beyond material and familial success toward more generative and caring institutions is the framework of call for Boomers.

For Boomers, how to recover (or find for the first time) a sense of wholeness and connection with a wider community beyond family often begins with searching for insight, for a spiritual practice that is different from what their parents had. In their search for an answer to *"What is my work?,"* Boomers are beginning to face the spiritual questions about meaning and service that come in the last half of life.

Busters, born 1965 - 1980

Born to Bridger and Boomer parents, Busters parallel the lower birthrate of the Bridger generation because birth-control is more widely available. This so-called "Generation X," who grew up with MTV and computers, eschews description and categorization. At home on the World Wide Web, they are well-educated but under-employed (because Boomers are already in those jobs), often unmarried but loyal to a small group of friends, suspicious of public institutions, and conscious of environmental degradation. Many have a global perspective through international travel, are resourceful and entrepreneurial, have faith in personal connections but little historical perspective.

Busters are looking for new forms of family and community, a few reliable relationships in a constantly changing world. Busters will volunteer their time to help out people in need, but those efforts need to be organized by somebody else and, for the most part, be short-term or one-time contributions. A typical scenario would be a group of friends who sign up to provide a Christmas party for needy kids at a neighborhood shelter but do who not want a more lasting commitment there.

The emerging model of church for Busters is a self-organizing unit, usually small in size and flexible enough to receive what they want to offer. They work hard, play hard, and reject formality. Establishing *"Who I am"* is the primary spiritual work for Busters as they enter a chaotic global village linked by the Internet.

Some writers add another generation, the so-called "13th Generation," born since 1980, but for the purpose of examining the cycles of call, I believe they will begin the process of searching for call by asking the same initial question as Busters, *"Who am I?"*

• THE SPIRAL PATH OF CALL •

At each stage of life—whether we are identifying self, work, gift, or legacy—when we complete the six-stage cycle of soulwork, we begin the cycle again. I think of call as a spiral path, circling around to start at a deeper place each time, with greater focus and more understanding of how we connect the temporal and eternal dimensions of life. In each round of the spiral journey, the focus and result will be different, depending on age and circumstances of our life.

The time between calls can be frightening and discouraging unless we know it is a natural part of the pattern. Each time we sense that a call has run its course, leaving us empty and bereft of purpose, we can trust that something new will arrive...because we have experienced this barren desert time before...because we know we are in the space between calls, when the whisper of purpose is too soft to hear. Each time we progress through the six stages of call, we learn more about how to listen for a new call. Experience with previous call may not necessarily make it easier to say "yes" to a new call, but each journey through the stages of call will build the qualities of soul necessary for the next round.

• • •

Before you continue reading about the cycle of call, I invite you to practice this simple thought experiment:

Sit quietly and focus on your breathing,
counting from one through four and then return to one,
while your mind rests with the question,
"What is my call now?"

• • •

The Cycle Of Call

CHAPTER 2

I noticed the candle first, small and bright beyond her dark profile. Then, through the great glass windows came the first hint of dawn. Our cook for the weekend sat perfectly still for the next hour as light slid noiselessly into the room, cradling the candle in brightness.

When the first rosy beams of sunlight touched the trees, she stood with a sigh and turned, nodding to me as she moved toward the kitchen. "I'm waiting for a new call," she said simply.

I knew she had been treated for cancer, had left her psychotherapy practice, and was cooking here to reclaim a simpler rhythm for her life. I learned later that she sat thus every morning, watching light overcome the darkness, listening for the still, small voice of God. It was her way of opening to God, of praying for a new direction.

Somewhere deep inside, we may recognize that our way of life is destroying our souls, along with the planet, and yet we feel powerless to change. We may feel enslaved but do not believe God has the power to change things, any more than we believe our institutions can save us. We may sense something inexorable is driving the global economy, but we do not know what to do about the destruction of local cultures and diverse beliefs. When we look closely, we may see our economic bondage and notice we do not feel a spiritual core that would give us a sense of freedom about our lives. We may no longer believe in heaven, so we spend our lives trying to create perfection on earth and blame others for the difficulties, accidents, and failures of human life.

The first step in recovering a sense of sacred purpose is to get quiet and to listen to the cry for help that comes from our souls. If we can learn to listen, we will hear a call, an invitation to meaning and purpose. We will discover a way to freedom that is both personal and systemic, part of the great liberation story for all of creation.

When we do hear the cry for meaning that comes from deep within, we may not know how to interpret the answering voice. There is an old story about the man who is hanging from a small root over a steep chasm, crying out for help. A voice from above answers, "Let go!" To which he replies, "Is anybody else up there?" Indeed, that is the dilemma of soulwork—we may not like the answer we hear when we cry for help.

One way in which we can practice listening for the voice of call is to read and understand the stories of those who have walked before us. I often go to biblical stories because so many of them describe people who have come to the end of their own answers. They offer clues about the ways in which oppression and struggle can be fertile ground for call. I have chosen two stories in particular for this book, one featuring Gideon, a male tribal warrior, and the other, a beautiful woman who became Queen Esther. Although they are set in different times and places and reveal entirely different circumstances, both stories illustrate the same underlying cycle of call that comes when we are ready, even if not quite willing.

We can approach these biblical stories on three different levels. The first level is *personal*. We can identify ourselves with the main character in each story, try on some of these situations to see whether they fit us today, and come to understand that the biblical story is really our story, too. The second level is *systemic*. We can look at the cultural dynamics, pay attention to power structures, and make connections with contemporary patterns that include some and exclude others. At that level, moral and ethical questions evolve, and we can explore what is being revealed about God's intention for human life. The third level is the *biblical/archetypal* level, in which certain themes and figures constellate energy from the collective unconscious. At this expansive mythical level, there is room for mystery and metaphor, for a God beyond our understanding but accessible through sign, symbol, and dreams.

• *GIDEON'S STORY* •

The biblical story of Gideon[1] begins with a clear cry for help from the Hebrew people, who are being persecuted by soldiers from Midian. The Midianites are so cruel that many Israelites have fled to the mountains where they are living in caves. They have been pleading for rescue, but God has been silent. Then a stranger appears among the downtrodden Hebrews, calling them to turn away from false gods. This prophet reminds them of God's power to deliver them from slavery in Egypt. His "otherness" signals the beginning of a new cycle—he is out of time and place, a *mysterious* figure. We are not told who the stranger is, but he is a messenger who calls the people of Israel to take notice. His appearance heralds the beginning of Gideon's call cycle.

Stage 1: RESIST

Following the appearance of this stranger, an angel appears to Gideon while he is threshing wheat in a winepress, a practice that kept the food a secret from the marauding Midianites. "The Lord is with you, mighty warrior," says the angel.

"Mighty warrior" hardly fits this hesitant and fearful man who is trying to eke out a living from the land. Gideon resists, pointing to the bad situation they are in as evidence of God's absence. When the angel persists, Gideon replies somewhat peevishly, "If the Lord is with us, why has all this happened to us? Where are all the wonders that our fathers told us about?" The angel ignores Gideon's complaint and reveals the mission God has in mind—that Gideon will lead an army against Midian.

"How can I possibly save Israel?" questions Gideon. "My clan is the weakest . . . and I am the least in my family." He denies his own gifts, hides in his helplessness, and refuses the call.

The angel seems to honor Gideon's resistance and challenge it at the same time. "Go in the strength you have," the angel tells Gideon, "Am I not sending you?" Gideon has lost all confidence in the presence or power of God flowing through the community, but the angel insists that God is the true Source, the sender. In his struggle to survive, Gideon's perspective would have to change before he would be able to move in a new direction. He would have to hear the call before he could respond to it.

Stage 2: RECLAIM

To reclaim the close relationship that Israel once had with God, Gideon would have to experience it himself. "Give me a sign that it is really God who is talking to me," Gideon says. "Wait here until I get an offering of food." For Gideon, offering traditional hospitality was a way to deepen the encounter and perhaps to remember stories of other angelic visitations to confirm the possibility that this could be a visitor from God.

"I will wait," the angel answers, signaling the reliability of this sacred dimension.

Stage 3: REVELATION

When Gideon returns with meat and bread, the angel tells him to put it on a rock and then, with the tip of a staff, touches the meat. Fire flares from the rock, consuming Gideon's offering in a dramatic revelation. The fire is a sign to Gideon that God is surely present, and Gideon is terrified, fearing that he will die from this encounter. The angel reassures Gideon that, like Moses before him, he will not die but, instead, can respond to the call that the angel is presenting.

As though to test Gideon's resolve and anchor this revelation in time and space, the angel directs Gideon to tear down his father's altar to Baal and build a proper one to God, then sacrifice a bull from his father's herd as a blood-offering to signify Gideon's commitment.

Knowing that he will surely be discovered, Gideon goes "by night" to carry out the angel's command. The next morning, a mob forms to hunt whoever has destroyed the altar to Baal. Finally they determine it must be Gideon, so they come to the house of Gideon's father, demanding that he turn the younger man over to them. Gideon's father refuses, saying "Let Baal punish the perpetrator," thus saving Gideon's life.

THE POISON RIVER

For Gideon, the consequence of tearing down his father's altar means that he cannot go back to being the innocent farmer he was when the call first came. The angel's fire and Gideon's response have brought him to a critical point in the call cycle, to the edge of the "Poison River." Seemingly ready to obey the angel, Gideon summons others to join him in fighting the Midianites. But as the guerrilla army of Israel begins to gather, Gideon suffers another surge of fear and indecision. This is the point when he could easily slip back into his old fearful self and begin the cycle again, going back to Stage One resistance.

The Cycle of CALL

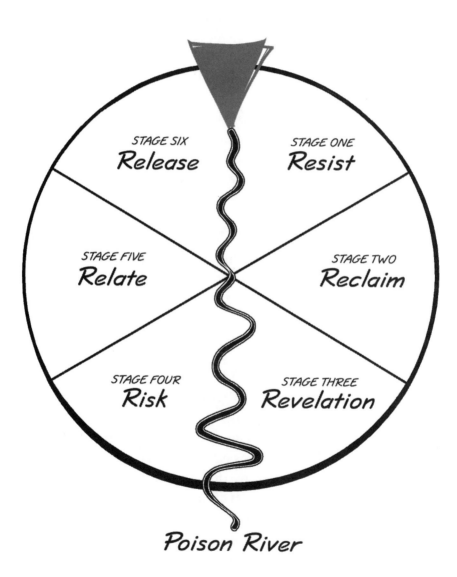

STAGE SIX
Release

STAGE ONE
Resist

STAGE FIVE
Relate

STAGE TWO
Reclaim

STAGE FOUR
Risk

STAGE THREE
Revelation

Poison River

Terrified that God does not have enough power to carry this challenge through to completion—or he afraid that he does not have the courage to respond as the warrior he is called to be—Gideon "throws a fleece" to test for God's presence. First, he asks God to put dew on a sheepskin and keep the surrounding ground dry. Then, to make absolutely certain, he asks God for the reverse. After this miraculous sign, Gideon is ready to act decisively. For Gideon, throwing the fleece marks the crossing point between dreaming of change and doing something about it.

Stage 4: RISK

At this point in the story, Gideon's relationship with God moves from angelic direction to direct intuition, as though Gideon has internalized the divine presence. God directs Gideon to prune the number of volunteer soldiers down, so they will not be fooled into thinking that victory is their own doing. For Gideon, the external risk is public humiliation—after all, what commander reduces his force just before battle? The internal risk is trusting God for the same kind of guidance that Moses received when he led the Israelites out of Egypt.

God's instructions are that anyone who trembles with fear should turn back. It is not difficult to see the allusion here. Fear is a sign that Gideon's warriors do not trust God and that old securities are still tugging back toward old answers. Warriors who have not crossed their own "Poison River" will be the first to go back home.

After this first pruning, there are still too many fighters to please God, so Gideon is instructed to take the remaining warriors down to a brook. Whoever laps water directly from the brook is to be sent home. Perhaps these are the very soldiers who would not be wary enough to survive the risks of war. This second round of pruning left Gideon with "a few good men," three hundred to be exact.

Then God provides Gideon with more reassurance: "If you are still afraid to attack, go into the camp of your enemies, and you will be encouraged." So Gideon sneaks into their camp and hears the Midianites talking about a dream in which the tent of their commander has been collapsed by a big rolling loaf of barley bread. The dream spreads fear among the enemy commanders because they sense the meaning: Because Israel serves as a source of food for Midian troops, the rolling loaf portends victory for Gideon's volunteer army.

Stage 5: RELATE

Reassured of God's presence by the dream, Gideon relates his personal guidance, takes public action, and trusts God for the wider consequences. He breaks his three-hundred men into three companies of one hundred each, arms them with a trumpet, a pitcher, and a candle, and sends them into battle position. These ritual objects are more like worship symbols than the tools of war. When the right moment comes, all three companies blow their trumpets, smash their pitchers, and raise their torches high as they shout. The enemy runs away in disgrace. Oh that it would be so easy in real life!

As the Hebrew warriors give chase to their fleeing foes, they fight with other Hebrew tribes who wanted to be part of the action. These arguments serve to reorganize the tribes of Abraham around Gideon's leadership. As the fighting ends, Gideon's leadership makes him a hero.

Stage 6: RELEASE

After the battle, the people react by trying to make Gideon their ruler. He wisely declines, telling them, "I will not rule over you, nor will my son. The Lord will rule over you." He resists the temptation to be their king and takes on the role of elder, patriarch of his clan.

In spite of his victory as a "mighty warrior," Gideon's real lesson was learning to trust the God who promised to go with him. Gideon claimed the call that came to him while he was threshing grain with a winepress, but as he lived through all six stages, his nature and his fears shaped the call just as much as the call shaped him.

During Gideon's lifetime, Israel continued to enjoy peace but "no sooner had Gideon died than the Israelites again prostrated themselves to the Baals," and the cycle began again. While Gideon seems to have experienced the deeper soulwork of each stage, his people have to begin another cycle after he dies.

• ESTHER'S STORY •

Queen Esther's story combines mythical and historical material. First recorded in both Greek and Hebrew about 300 B.C. in the Hellenistic period, the story is set 250 years earlier during the Babylonian Exile, when the Jews were taken away from their homeland. I like to use the more descriptive Greek version of Esther's story as told in *The Jerusalem Bible.*[2] There the story begins when Esther's cousin, Mordecai, dreams of two dragons battling. Their fury destroys everything in their path. Then, from the ground comes a cry for help! The cry becomes a stream and finally a mighty river that swallows the two dragons. The text says, "Mordecai walked around all day, wondering what the dream could mean."

Mordecai learns that the King's chief counselor, Haman, has persuaded the King to issue an edict against the Jews because they refuse to worship the King as a god. Haman knows that Mordecai is a Jew, but he does not suspect that the Queen is Jewish because Mordecai has sworn her to secrecy about her background. Mordecai himself becomes a sign of distress, a call for help, by dressing in sackcloth and ashes to signify mourning and placing himself before the palace where Esther can see him.

Stage 1: RESIST

Esther does not want to know what is wrong. She resists Mordecai's cry for help and sends a servant out with fresh clothes for him. If she were to claim her relationship with Mordecai, it would reveal her identity as a Jew, so she turns away from whatever need his mortification portends.

Mordecai then becomes the messenger of God's call, asking Queen Esther to enter the King's chamber to beg for the reversal of the edict he has issued against the Jews. Like the angel who addressed Gideon as "mighty warrior," Mordecai demands of Esther a level of courage and public action that she cannot imagine for herself. She, too, is out of touch with God's presence and power. Esther resists, saying, "The King has not asked for me in thirty days." In other words, she has no special claim on the King's favor, and she is afraid to go to him.

Stage 2: RECLAIM

Mordecai warns Esther that she will not escape the edict against the Jews just because she is in the King's palace. "If you persist in remaining silent . . . relief and deliverance will come from another place," he says with a threatening tone. He challenges her to reclaim her identity as a Jew—even risk death for the deliverance of her people—in order to draw from the power of God's presence.

Stage 3: REVELATION

"Who knows?" Mordecai adds. "Perhaps you have come to the throne for just such a time as this." Mordecai's question reveals a larger purpose to Esther. Has she been placed in the court to deliver her people? Is there a call for her in Mordecai's request? Esther must decide whether to obey her instinct to hold on to her silence, pretending she does not have a connection with Mordecai, or to prepare herself for the dangerous mission ahead.

THE POISON RIVER

Mordecai's question seems to call forth Esther's inner knowing that she is, indeed, born for just such a time as this. She plunges into the unknown when she sends a message back to Mordecai through her servant, saying "Tell the Jews to fast and pray for three days, and I will do the same." She knows she cannot face this trial on her own willpower. She is willing but afraid, so she retreats to make contact with a power greater than herself.

Symbolically, Esther enters the "Poison River" when she strips off her royal robes to fast and pray for three days. She humbles her body and soul, bereft of earthly symbols of power, to test her relationship with God. She cries out to God for courage and guidance in these prophetic words from the Greek translation: ". . . come to my help, for I am alone and have no helper but you and am about to take my life in my hands."

Stage 4: RISK

When her "retreat" is over, Esther puts on her royal robes and her crown, as though to remind the King of their relationship. Externally, she risks her life by coming to the King's chambers when she has not been summoned. Internally, she decides to trust the guidance she believes will come from God as she takes each step.

The Greek version says, "His face blazed with anger," but when Esther begins to faint, the King leaps to her side and begs to know what has caused her to risk her life. Then, in what seems to be a ridiculously small request, Esther invites the King and her enemy, Haman, to a private dinner that she will prepare with her own hands. Stripped down to the essential reliance on her connection with Spirit, Esther takes a first small step toward a much larger mission.

Stage 5: RELATE

Esther stays in deep communion with divine guidance and with her particular sphere of influence, Haman and the King. Because she has not received guidance to move ahead, she does nothing at the dinner party but invite Haman and the King back the next night. Esther knows it is not yet God's *kairos* time to make her request on behalf of her people.

Between the first and second banquets, Haman is humiliated into honoring his enemy Mordecai for discovering a plot against the King's life. Then, when Haman and the King join Esther for dinner in her royal quarters, the King promises Esther whatever she wants, "up to half my kingdom." She asks for "my life and that of my people."

The King is ready to grant her request, but he is shocked to discover that he himself is the one who has signed their death warrant. He cannot undo his own edict. As an immediate response, he has Haman hanged on the gallows originally built for Mordecai, but the edict against the Jews still stands.

Months later, Esther claims her relationship with the King once again and enters his chamber unbidden. This time she begs that the Jews be allowed to attack their foes on a particular day. Although the King cannot rescind his own order, he can allow the Jews the right to defend themselves. Esther asks for a second day of slaughter in the capital city, and that too is granted. The balance of power shifts, but this is no civil war. The battles are boundaried by time and place. It is an internal rearrangement. The King remains in charge, but Mordecai replaces Haman as the King's chancellor, and Esther has succeeded in relating her personal power not only with the political realm of the King but also with the larger spiritual realm of God.

Stage 6: RELEASE

At this point, Esther seems to have completed her part in God's story of deliverance. She releases her hold on history, seeming to disappear from view as the story comes to a close. In the Greek version, Mordecai goes back to his dream and says, "Now I understand. Haman and I were the dragons and Esther, the river between." Mordecai sees that he and Haman represented two different warring systems and, as Queen, Esther was the agent of God's deliverance. The King was simply the framework for their conflict, not the opponent.

• • •

In both of these biblical stories, just one cycle of call is fully described, but we know that the stories are part of an ongoing process by which the nature of God is revealed through the Judeo-Christian tradition. Gideon's story is part of the mythic past before King David united the tribes of Israel and Judah into one kingdom centered around Jerusalem. In Jewish congregations, Esther's story is still celebrated today as Purim, a kind of "Mardi Gras melodrama" of the triumph of good over evil.

• *THE SOULWORK CYCLE* •

The soulwork cycle always begins with a willingness to stop, look, and listen for our call. A cry for help comes from inside or out—a stranger arrives, a familiar friend assumes different garb, sickness becomes a sign that all is not well. Like Esther and Gideon, we may resist at first, but gradually, as the call unfolds and we test its authenticity, we come to the river of no return. Opposition and challenge become allies as we choose to trust eternal guidance. As we name each stage of this soulwork cycle and claim the learnings there, call moves from the private inner space of inspiration and intuition into the outer field of action and interaction where social systems bind us together as a people. We risk failure with few resources but choose to act anyway. Then in the last two stages of the cycle, we broaden the experience of call by sharing it, building some kind of social organization in which others have a crucial role in giving our call form and substance in the world.

Stage One: RESIST

CHAPTER 3

I feel anxious and unsettled. Nothing satisfies my vague sense of hunger. I feel a change coming but am too tired to care. My dreams are disturbing. I believe they hold an invitation to new birth, but I am not ready to shift my priorities. I've stopped writing in my journal regularly and can't seem to find the energy or willpower I need right now. I feel like a slug. My body is hanging onto old forms even as my soul grows restless, yearns for something else. I can't figure out how to make space for it.

The first sign of Stage One is resistance to the idea that we might be called to a larger purpose in life. resistance always tugs against recognition. A messenger arrives—in our bodies or our dreams, through a psychic break or a failure in the external world. Something comes unbidden to signal that all is not well. Or, just when we feel totally abandoned, something happens to remind us of our relationship with the universe. Serendipities occur. A coincidence or sign catches our attention. We hear a story that resonates with rightness or see a rainbow or catch sight of a bird in high flight.

The soulwork cycle begins with a visceral response. As an organism, we seek homeostasis, stability, and balance. Biologically we are built to survive and deep change feels threatening, so our first reaction to call is denial. Like Gideon and Esther, we resist these messengers of call, preferring our own methods of coping with whatever difficulties life seems to have for us. We resist giving ourselves to the unknown and cling to what we know.

Resistance implies a boundary between different states of matter, otherness, opposing forces, friction, attraction without absorption. All boundaries have a purpose. Resistance provides us with a dynamic screen for discerning what is and is not call. In fact, exploring our resistance is really the only way to begin to explore our call. Only by leaning into our place of resistance—by paying attention to images, dreams, or recurrent patterns of worry or anger—can we open ourselves to a new awareness. Entering the muddy waters of soulwork is not so much a movement toward ecstatic fusion with God as it is recognizing the downward and inward presence of God in earthy clay and ordinary moments.

• *FORMS OF RESISTANCE* •

I find it comforting that Elizabeth O'Connor, one of the "saints" at The Church of the Saviour who wrote and spoke about call for many years, was willing to admit the depth of her hesitation. In her book *Cry Pain, Cry Hope*, she explored her resistance—which for her took the form of five years of physical illness—to what she *knew* to be a call to write a book. In her journal she wrote: "Partly I am undone by what I feel to be the expectations of others. I think that, if I set aside a portion of my day for writing, at the end of that day some evidence of my industry will be demanded of me . . . It is as

Stage 1: Resist

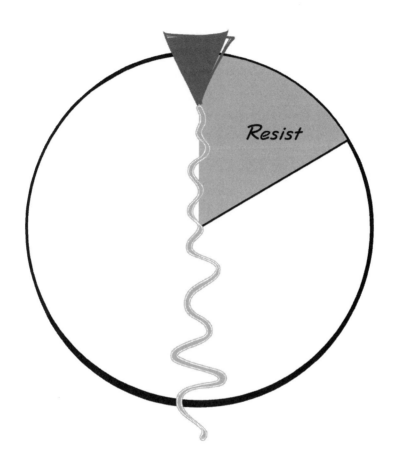

though I am slave labor—back in Egypt building tombs." [1] She imagined that her friends had become overseers, requiring some accounting of her time. In another place, she wrote, "Is this God at work tearing down those things that have made me feel self-sufficient, helping me to move toward the experience of nothingness of which the saints write, the meaning of which is so hard to grasp?" She named self-sufficiency as the block to her call, detailing diversions and wondering out loud if her illness was a signal that God was calling her to a new work. [2]

For me, resistance to the stirring of a new call usually takes the form of forgetfulness: I leave my purse behind, forget appointments, and generally exhibit signs of distraction. As though my soul is already busy with something else, I am not fully present in the moment. I may be aware of feeling somewhat lost and disoriented, confused about what to do next, but having been well-trained in cultural compensation, I usually forge ahead and take on new responsibilities, ignoring my feelings of uncertainty. Feelings of tiredness and frustration surface, and I am likely to take chances with my driving, drop things in the kitchen, have little "accidents." I feel numb and dumb, with a physical sensation of being frozen. I feel far from the spark of life that burns at the core of my being.

In truth, a new call terrifies me. When I get a sense of a new call, I harbor a wish to fit it in with what I am already doing. But I cannot because my life is already overfull, and I do not want the work of shifting my priorities to make space for the unknown. I deny my failure to acknowledge a new call and keep this secret urge to myself, without naming it. I do not know what to say. I "forget" to speak about it with friends. Thoughts tumble and refuse to stay ordered. I behave like a shock victim because I am afraid of change, am addicted to my comforts, and like the patterns I have constructed to keep anxiety at bay. I cannot get my mind around the new input, so I hang onto the patterns that have kept me going and hide behind my busyness like a child: "I can't . . . I'm too busy . . . if only you knew what I've been through . . . " I resist—and only notice when things begin to fall apart or fail.

In contrast to my circuitous approach, my octogenarian friend M. C. Richards is someone who does not seem to resist call at all. She lives wide open to her cosmic connections, ready to embrace whatever comes her way. She trusts her feelings and lets them guide her toward radical newness. Interested first in language, she got a Ph.D. in literature from Berkeley. Then she became a potter, letting the metaphor of centering on a potter's wheel become the focus of her book *Centering in Pottery, Poetry, and the Person.* Now she is painting from her center—unschooled, full of color, filled with Spirit. Her latest book of poetry offers a sense of mystery even in the title: *Imagine Inventing Yellow!* But M.C. tells a story of illness that plagued her for several years until she realized that she had "no resistance" to the disabling virus that had entered her system. "To resist the virus, I had to say NO! Push back. Stop giving in to it," she said.[3] Her body seemed to be telling her to set some limits. Developing resistance marked a new beginning for her.

M.C.'s story brings to mind the image of a potter's wheel where resistance is a centering pressure of hand against clay, drawing the expansive force of the spinning wheel inward with centripetal force so the molecules of clay can rearrange themselves, find their own pattern of fit in a smooth mound of readiness. Though the experience of call may come from an outside source, we feel both its expansiveness and our resistance as internal conflict. The role of resistance is to help us sort out the pressures and organize a response from within. Although we are familiar with instant fight-or-flight physical responses to perceived dangers, we are less acquainted with the slower rhythms of soul in response to genuine call, where resistance can help rearrange the very substance of our lives.

We resist giving ourselves fully to the unknown because, when we do, we feel so naked and vulnerable, childlike and dependent on something beyond ourselves. Even if our childhood experience of dependence on adults has been good, when we grow up we "put away childish things" and act as though we should be able to start new things without falling into the abyss of unknowing. To engage our stubborn core of resistance, we must be willing to enter a time of "not knowing" that goes against our cultural patterns of reason, autonomy, and control.

At the same time, to resist "not knowing" is both a sign of new birth and of healthy caution. Symbolized in mythology by a trip to the underworld, or time in the tomb, or forty days in the desert, genuine call is a fearful thing, worthy of our resistance!

• *SUBSTITUTES* •

Because opening to a new call means shedding some basic organizing patterns, leaving us (for a time) in a raw state of feeling, resistance can be a healthy sign of call. Some people shut down or deaden themselves with obsessive activity, drink, or drugs. Others reach for a substitute—something or someone who is closer and more tangible, more real than the mysterious sense of connection to what is universal. For many of us, the closest thing to call is "falling in love," hard. We may feel drawn to someone who, on the surface, may not seem a likely partner but who, in some way, carries part of our call in a visible form. Our culture honors that "fatal attraction." Movies and television glorify emotional entanglements. However, obsessive attraction can be a sign of deeper call—if we have the wit to explore it further. But many of us fall into the easy habit of thinking about what we deserve instead of asking deeper questions of purpose and call.

In Stage One, we sometimes substitute the feeling of attraction for the deeper challenge of call. We see in someone else an image or reflection of what we ourselves could embody. Not only is this a common pattern for women who are attracted to the power traditionally exercised by men in our society, but also for men who resist developing relational skills traditionally claimed by women. We sometimes marry the gifts we are meant to develop in ourselves, but the cult of happiness makes a poor substitute for purpose. If we do not do the inner work of reclaiming disowned parts of ourselves, this form of attraction will not last.

Even though a substitute for call can only satisfy us temporarily, who or what we choose can be another clue to the call itself. Harville Hendricks, author of *Getting the Love You Want*, has founded a school of Imago Therapy based on the premise that we are attracted to the very person who, in a conscious relationship, can be the agent for healing the wounds we grew up with. Beyond the feeling level of attraction, Hendricks suggests we can discover the presence of call in the heart of every intimate relationship because we are drawn to those who carry lost parts of who we are meant to be. I would go one step further and propose that we are also drawn to people who can call us to the work we are here to do. We envy, admire, and very often avoid the people who are living out the call we carry inside. The feelings are complex but the attraction is strong because we are meant to learn more about the purpose this person carries for us. Either avoidance or obsessive attraction can be a sign of resisting call.

• THE INNOCENT RESISTS •

In the first stage of call, we live with the tension of trusting the universe and being receptive to call, while at the same time being suspicious and drawing back from the call. Carol Pearson, in her book *Awakening the Heroes Within,* identifies these two positions as the Innocent and the Orphan, two of twelve archetypal inner guides for the soul's archetypal journey.[4]

The Innocent is a perfectionist, clinging tightly to "oughts" and "shoulds." He has a blaming voice, sure of how things are "supposed" to be: what God is supposed to do, how others are supposed to act, how healthy or protected or simple our lives "should" be. This is exactly what Gideon did in the biblical story when he questioned the angel who appeared to him. His initial response was the resistant cry of the Innocent: "If the Lord is with us, why has all this happened to us?" In Gideon's mind, things were not the way they were supposed to be! He clung to a preconceived picture of what he thought God ought to do and blamed God for not making it happen. He questioned the call and the caller, pointing to the situation as evidence of God's absence.

The Innocent believes the world is a safe place just waiting to be explored and that others are there to help and save him when he gets into trouble. Ever the optimist, the Innocent carries an idealized picture not only of himself, but of others. Trust and interdependence come easily for him. When pushed, he idealizes and then blames others for not living up to their potential.

If we are perfectionistic, one way of coping with a rapidly changing environment is to make the sphere of our decisions very small, narrow the realm of control down to something we can handle, and simply ignore or criticize the larger currents of change swirling around us, blaming our leaders, friends, or any other convenient target. Gideon's behaviors were those of a classic Innocent: he hid himself in his clan (the weakest in Israel) and family (the least of his clan), as well as in his people's history as victims of the Midianites. He believed he was powerless to change things . . . and that God was powerless to change things. Caught in his struggle to survive, Gideon resisted a more heroic and difficult role for himself.

The shadow side of perfectionism is projected hostility, where we demonize "the enemy" instead of seeing evil as part of creation and part of ourselves. The Innocent resists knowledge of evil, of complexity, of ambiguity and paradox. The Innocent imagines he can keep the darker themes of soulwork from his conscious mind and be dedicated to workplace proficiency instead. In classic Innocent fashion, Gideon blamed God for the situation of servitude to Midian instead of accepting responsibility for his people's substitution of other, more tangible, gods.

The Innocent also wants rescue. The passive expectation that the universe will somehow take care of us is a powerful temptation that we see acted out in countless ways. Women take on the Damsel-in-Distress guise, looking around for some Knight to save her. Men take on the Silent Stoic stance, as though endurance alone will be rewarded. Clothed in resistance, men often have to wait for a heart attack to break through the armor they have been schooled to wear. My Twelve-Step friends call this kind of innocence "the myth of terminal specialness"—the notion that somehow we are different, unique, not subject to normal consequences, or are at least deserving of parental rescue.

Another form of the Innocent is the optimist who sees how other people could be if only they would do things differently. This often happens when one person in a marriage does not want to know what the other is really like, when he or she would rather hang on to an idealized picture than deal with the evidence of the spouse's true nature. You can hear this when someone says " . . . but he's got so much potential" or "It just happened once; it won't happen again." When our powers of denial are greater than our capacity for truth, we may be stuck in Stage One for a long time. This is not unlike Gideon and his people who fell into the trap of thinking that God would always rescue them because they were special and chosen. The Innocent waits for a savior.

In America, the Builder generation tried to provide an experience of happy innocence for their postwar Boomer children because they themselves had grown up in a simpler era, with small-town habits of trust and optimism, and they wanted to protect their children from the terrors of Depression and world war. Even today, Builders and their Boomer children bring an attitude of innocence and optimism to deeper questions of internal evil and external consequences. Like Gideon, they tend to trust that, in the end, somebody or something will come along and save them.

The current popularity of angel books and angel shows on television suggests that we are largely a nation of Innocents longing for God to rescue us from the human condition. At a feeling level, angel shows give us a picture of celestial beings who want to give us protection in a dangerous world. We want sweetness and light. We want rescue, and in so doing, we neglect the mystery of God in other forms—the long, slow rhythms of the earth needed to make clay from stone, the wonder and terror of vast space, the destructive consequences of global markets, the reality of disability and death as a part of the larger life cycle,

The answer that the popular media seems to be giving to our spiritual hunger is that God will go to great lengths to save individuals from their own stupidity and disbelief, that miracles do occur, and that love is finally what we all need to give and receive. This certainly is part of the picture of call—but not all of it.

The biblical picture of call frequently begins with an angel who comes saying, "Fear not, for behold . . . " These very words signal that the message angels deliver is one of challenge and of change that may even be life-threatening. Protection for our innocence is not usually part of the bargain. Biblical angels are not like the Publisher's Clearinghouse Sweepstakes with a lifetime-income prize. Until we get beyond the fixation on personal salvation and understand the context for our lives in a bigger cosmic sense, our notion of call will be small and limited to personal satisfaction.

One way the Innocent attempts to preserve his old conceptual framework in the face of a call is to question the source. In the early days of his career, Bill Cosby had a wonderful comic routine about Noah hearing God's call to build an ark. After what seemed like crazy commands coming from this cavernous voice in the sky, Noah blurts out, "Who are you . . . really?" Noah wanted to know if this was some kind of practical joke: "Are we on Candid Camera? What kind of God would be asking me to build an ark when the skies are clear?"

In similar fashion, Gideon responded to his visitor, questioning what kind of God this was. Why, if God was so powerful, were things so bad? In Gideon's mind, God was supposed to be like a good parent, protective and tolerant. Gideon blamed God for their situation and resisted taking any responsibility himself. We do the same when we question why God would let *that* (illness, accident, Holocaust) happen! Blaming God as a parental figure questions the source of call . . . but it still leaves room for new understanding. Ultimately, our relationship with the Divine Source has to change, and we have to "grow up" before we can respond to the call to take responsibility for our part in God's ongoing creation.

• *THE ORPHAN RESISTS* •

If the Innocent is an idealist, then the Orphan is a realist. Knowing that Esther was an orphan, brought up by her cousin, helps us understand her resistance. When Mordecai asked her to plead her people's case before the King, Esther assessed her chances for survival and initially said, "No. The King has not asked for me in thirty days." She knew that she would be risking death if she went to the King without an invitation and he did not feel like granting her special dispensation. Esther refused to risk her position in the court. She rejected her power to persuade just because she was the Queen. *Realpolitik* was natural for her.

The Orphan is not so likely to question the identity of the caller as she is to question her own identity. This is exactly what Esther did when faced with Mordecai's request. Instead of asking, "Who are you . . . really?" her unspoken question was, "Who am *I* . . . really?" Realizing that her identity and access were dependent upon the King's favor, Esther denied Mordecai's request. She was neither a fool nor a martyr.

This self-reliance may stem from the Orphan's early experience with abandonment, being psychologically (or physically) orphaned and left alone to fend for oneself. Cast out of her clan and family, forbidden to speak of her heritage when she was chosen to be the Queen of Babylon, and made ritually unclean by her intimacy with a foreign king, Esther would always be an outcast from her people. She had to depend upon herself and her silent relationship with God to remember who she was, without the mirror of her culture or her kind.

If the Innocent is a perfectionist, then the Orphan is a pragmatist, testing every intimation of call against the practical questions of survival and stability. The Orphan is suspicious and calculating. She may even appear cold and distant, self-sufficient and unlikely to trust easily. Instead of optimism, the Orphan is prone to pessimism: "It will never work"; "I can't see how the situation will ever change"; "Nobody really cares." The Orphan lives with chronic feelings of scarcity, no matter how many things she has. Conscious of her separateness, her essential aloneness, the Orphan seeks to control her environment because she does not trust anyone else to care for her. Even if she is a person of faith, she does not really trust God's care or provision.

Just as the Innocent is inclined to project his call on another, falling in love with the qualities he is supposed to birth in himself, the Orphan is more inclined to look inward and seek her insights alone. Fear of abandonment shades every relationship for the Orphan, who is more likely to withdraw into depression and self-examination (sometimes obsessively) for her answers. For the Orphan, resistance buys time to find her own solutions.

If the Orphan's fear of abandonment is stronger than early experiences of care and nurture, disillusionment comes easily and trust will be harder. The Orphan may fear exploitation and victimization, but learns early to "stand on her own two feet" and grab what she can. A major drawback for the Orphan is that she may refuse help because her habits of self-reliance are so strong. While the Orphan has the capacity for strong peer relationships with other independent souls, she may not be able to bond deeply enough for true interdependence.

According to Madonna Kolbenschlag in *Lost in the Land of Oz*, the Orphan often distrusts and circumvents authority figures, but can develop strong peer relationships with other independent people. Kolbenschlag points to the great migrations of refugees in the world today as evidence that this is the primary archetype in modern society. Unconscious innocence is gone, she says, but the result is not necessarily a nation of rebels and outcasts. Orphans can learn to be conscious of being singular parts of a greater whole —which is the essence of call in the biblical model.[5]

Marketing and advertising of products rely heavily on the Orphan's need for reassurance. Trying to enhance who we are is central to the form of capitalism practiced in America. Eric Hoffer, the philosopher who worked as a longshoreman, is said to have remarked, "We can never get enough of what we do not really want."

At some level, we know that material things will not fulfill us, but without the security of a family or society to protect our innocence, the Orphan adapts to what is available and develops strong habits of self-reliance. While the Innocent looks for a rescuer, the Orphan relies on her own resourcefulness for a solution, as Esther did.

In America today, people of the Bridger generation, shaped by Depression and World War II, are figurative, if not literal, orphans. They grew up essentially orphaned by the war, even when their fathers came home safely afterward. The Orphan mentality of the Bridgers is being repeated in the lives of their Buster children. Busters grew up feeling abandoned by society in which divorce, drugs, and violence were commonplace. Both Bridgers and Busters are more typically Orphan-types, more at home with a culture that has shifted from the church-oriented society of the fifties to a secular world without unconscious community. Loneliness feels familiar, though not comfortable.

Both Bridgers and Busters are more likely to look for answers within, creating alliances with a pragmatic purpose, accepting their own skepticism and choosing to act anyway because they are realists, not idealists. Even if they have achieved considerable wealth and status, Bridgers and Busters tend to resist a new call by turning inward, embracing the practice of meditation, long-distance running or biking, solitary and entrepreneurial efforts to change the surrounding culture.

While self-doubt may shadow the Orphan's decision, Orphan qualities may also aid the search for call because they develop reliance on internal guidance. Some of these positive qualities emerge in Esther's story. She was able to keep her Jewish heritage a secret when she entered the royal harem. She was self-contained and self-reliant, and later was able to draw strength from her early experience when facing a life-threatening situation—she had "been there" before and found ways to survive without the surrounding affirmation of her culture. Esther found a way to be "at home" in a foreign land and an alien culture, attentive to the cues from others about how to survive and thrive there. Unlike Gideon, Esther did not spend time bemoaning how life "ought" to be. Her beliefs about herself and her world were based on more realistic circumstances.

• *BEGINNER'S MIND* •

We each contain both Innocent and Orphan. We all start out as Innocents with some cellular memory of the womb where every need was met—the Garden of Eden at the dawn of our physical creation. Our bodies remember what Eden feels like, and at some level we yearn for that blissful state of union with God all through life. We want that nourishment; we long for loving touch and total acceptance. Without a way to return to this initial state of Oneness, we can be cynical, suspicious loners, cut off from God and one another. Life then becomes a win/lose proposition without an underlying basis for trust.

During adolescence, most of us play with the magical thinking that goes with extended innocence. We can be careless and daring, unable to believe that we will sicken or die. We do not want to grow up and deal with the paradox of good and evil intertwined. Instead, we bifurcate existence into "reality"—where evil lurks and we must go with our guard up—and "spirituality"—where there is an idealized state of blissful unity with the Divine. Separating body and spirit is one way of holding onto the possibility of union with God and, at the same time, dealing with the "realities" of living in a flawed world. We split sacred and secular apart, draining the sense of magic and mystery from our daily lives and dulling our Innocent's perception of the whole in every particular part.

If we have split our lives into separate compartments, reserving spiritual matters for private and personal times, we unlearn a child's innocent trust of basic body-knowing and connection with things outside of ourselves. Most of us, in fact, do not trust our intuitions and observations in the spiritual realm. We live in an age of specialization and have, until recently, left the cosmic framework to scientists and theologians. Generally, we do not have places where it is safe to ask questions, follow our leadings, test them with a like-minded community. We resist knowing the very thing that will free the creative powers in us. Like Gideon or Esther, we really do not want to hear a call because it means changing known patterns of life, comfortable because they are familiar.

In the midst of change, we need a "beginner's mind" to reconnect with a primal state of innocence that can form the basis for trust and reliability, hopefulness and optimism. We need to find a place of trust, even serenity, a stance of willingness to accept life as it is, not as we want it to be. Only then can we gain the perspective to recognize resistance as the skin of old concepts stretched thin by a new call growing inside.

At the core, listening for call is about restoring our relationship with self, with the world around us, and with God. Whatever brings us to back to the core experience of trust in life itself can be a starting point for hearing call. Many people have discovered that massage and meditation can be a receptive state of trust and safety. The recent popularity of centering prayer and Buddhist meditation suggest that we are learning to trust our body wisdom as a way to access Eden and the Innocent's way. To focus on our breathing and let our rational minds rest from the persistent problem-solving that is the pattern of our culture is a practice available to everyone. I call it "practicing Sabbath." It is the mark of a free person to set aside other people's expectations, to breathe and BE, in the midst of a frenzied field of competing demands.

Elizabeth O'Connor, writing about call in *Faith@Work* magazine in 1963, spoke about the "journey inward" as a source of guidance.[6] I sensed that she meant something quite different from the long list of things that I wanted to bring to God's attention in prayer. By the time I arrived at her church in 1976, I was not surprised to learn that one of the regular disciplines of The Church of the Saviour was silent retreat—a weekend without talk in the company of others from your worshipping community. The first time I went on a silent retreat, I took several books because I could not imagine how I might otherwise pass the time. Our retreat leader asked us to "lock any books you might have brought in your car" and suspend expectations about our time together. I was stunned!

Over the course of the weekend, I began to feel what she was inviting us to experience. Setting aside the language of words, I was able to notice other forms of connection and pay attention to my feelings more easily. Each meal required a sensitivity to one another that we did not usually practice. After eating, we sat in silent meditation with the group for at least an hour, simply aware of our breathing. Then we had a short reading or reflection poem to focus on and were free to roam outside or stay by the fire inside. It was a simple experience but the effects were profound. I felt more refreshed than if I had gone on vacation. Later I realized that I had been able to move through my fears without effort and drink deeply of the goodness that was there.

With time, I began to realize that I could experience that kind of "Sabbath" in other settings as well. Alone, I could breathe and sink into a state of rest that helped me connect with the *kairos* realm of God's ongoing creation story and feel included in the vastness of the night sky. With others, particularly during extended silence during worship, I could begin to feel the Innocent's ability to trust, to love, and to live with hope for a way through the chaos that is so prevalent in modern culture.

• BEYOND RESISTANCE •

For the Orphan, the world is an unsafe place where nourishment and protection must be sought every day; nothing is achieved without a struggle, and danger is always lurking. It is only when we can put our conscious selves in touch with the Innocent that we can move to the next stage of the soulwork cycle. When innocence is part of the mix we bring into adult life, then there is the possibility we can let old images of God as eternal parent crack wide open, and we can see new forms of relationship emerge.

That does not mean there is no room for the Orphan, for without the corrective edge of the Orphan's realism, the Innocent's idealism can lead to sentimentality and self-centeredness, as though human life and comfort were the only consideration in making decisions about how we are to live. But if we are controlled by the suspicious Orphan who fears change, it will be hard to believe there is anyone "out there" to trust.

For the Orphan, moving beyond resistance means identifying with a larger reality than self. For the Innocent, moving beyond resistance means confronting the reality of evil, of our mortality and limitations. Both are necessary if we are to move into Stage Two of the soulwork cycle.

Stage Two: RECLAIM

CHAPTER 4

At the time of my father's death in 1987, I spent some months with a dance therapist who helped me "get out of my head" and into my body. One day after watching me move about the room in silence with my eyes closed, she remarked, "You aren't using the space behind you."

She was right. I was not using the space behind me. Or the time. That's why I had come. With my father's death, I felt adrift, ungrounded. Her observation gave me a name for it: I had lost my past. Not literally, of course, but something about my father's death had shut down access to my intuition, and I knew it would take movement rather than words to reconnect.

Regardless of the form our resistance in Stage One takes—whether *denying* our own strengths or relying *solely* on our own strengths—the work of Stage Two is to reclaim from the unconscious collective of past associations who we truly are. We need to discover a larger context for our lives, reconnect with family and tradition, reclaim "the sacred." We will have to recall past connections, reweave the story of past history, and recover gifts that connect us to family, to work, to nature, to God. In Stage Two, we seek the form behind our skills—the original seed of call, the DNA of our souls. We may have to reenter dark places to face some of the dragons we needed to flee at earlier times and to reclaim powers that we can use now. We must gather and reassemble beliefs that expand our sense of meaning and purpose, even when we are fearful of taking the next step. While Stage One is largely an individual experience of response to call, Stage Two is primarily relational and communal, even as call begins to differentiate us from the herd.

For Gideon, awakening his relationship with his Source began with God's assurance through the angel, "I will be with you." Though Gideon did not trust those words, he was willing to test them by asking the angel to wait while he went to get some food. For Esther, reconnection with her past, her people, and with God began with Mordecai's warning: "Don't think your position will save you," he cautioned, "and if you persist in remaining silent, God will find another way." Esther's heightened awareness that she could not escape death awakened the story she had kept secret.

For me, it took the dance therapist's witness and reflection back in words to realize what I was missing. She helped me with an important part of reclaiming—reaching back for those times when someone noticed who I truly was. I am reminded of the words of Jungian analyst James Hillman, in his book *The Soul's Code*:

> Reading backward means that growth is less the key bio-graphical term than form, and that development only makes sense when it reveals a facet of the original image.[1]

As Hillman suggests, we need others who will reflect back to us our true nature so we can "read our lives backward" and discern the meaning and purpose more clearly. Those people do not need to be constants in our lives, but they do need to be there if we are to see the underlying form of who we are intended to be in different phases of life. Hillman talks about the "acorn" of call that is born into each person, something that must be born into the world through us. This kernel of call is tough and persistent, not easily blocked or dissipated. Speaking out against the psychologists who assume we are basically shaped from external forces, Hillman focuses his attention on the "soul's code," which is inborn and determined to manifest against all odds. If each of us has a "code" that shapes our unique soul, then our lifelong spiritual quest is to recognize and live out that purpose. It means we will have to find or create the web of relationships in which we can act from a core of healthy self-love, or live in angry frustration.

My father had often mirrored my "original image," and, with his death, I had to claim it for myself. Because the seed of my authentic self was largely preverbal and embodied, I could not *think* my way to it alone. The therapist's gift to me was seeing, naming, and knowing something of what my movement pattern meant. She invited memories of times when someone truly *saw* me and did not try to make me into a carbon copy of others for the sake of order or their convenience. She encouraged language for what had been unconscious, not just the personal past represented by my father, but my roots in a spiritual tradition and, ultimately, my relationship with God. She helped me "use the space behind" and rejoin past with present.

• *MASKS & MIRRORS* •

Reclaiming the seeds of soul from the dustbin of diversions requires a relationship with someone who can reflect back essential qualities. Mirroring and companionship are essential for reclaiming forgotten facets of the wholeness we were born with.

Stage 2: Reclaim

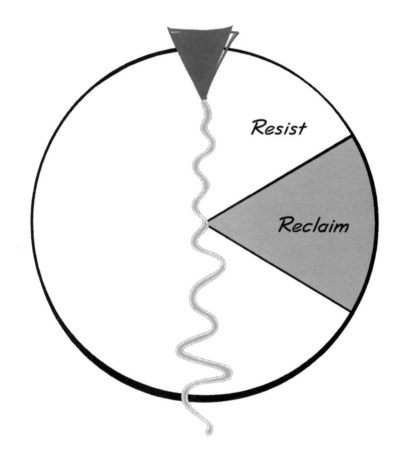

For Esther, her cousin Mordecai became her mirror. Her mask had been her beauty: She "passed" in a foreign culture because she fit some cultural definition of attractiveness and it gained her a position of power in the court. By reminding her that she would not escape the edict of the King against the Jews just because she was the Queen, Mordecai helped Esther begin to reclaim her identity as a Jew. He mirrored her true identity at a time when she wanted to deny it. He reminded her of her roots and her spiritual tradition.

Gideon, on the other hand, wore the mask of a docile farmer as he ground his grain in a winepress to keep it from marauding troops. The angel held up the mirror of his true identity as a "mighty warrior" and was willing to wait for Gideon to discover his capacity for call and partnering with God.

Early in life, we learn to mask who we are because it does not seem safe to do otherwise. Before we have the language or mental constructs to name what we know or defend who we are, much of our vitality is wrapped up in our physicality. At that stage, adults approve an adaptive persona, one that fits what the adults want. In her book *The Drama of the Gifted Child*, Alice Miller describes the adjustment that children begin to make toward accommodating their caregivers from the very beginning. Few parents have enough perspective to love without needing something from the child. They are either too close and too needy, or too distant to care and still let the child have space to be themselves. Caregivers, Miller proposes, often need a certain response for themselves."[2] Precious indeed is the adult who can mirror the reality of the child's nature, fanning the flame of spirit so it burns brightly, drawing out the special qualities that are there.

When we reach young adulthood and grapple with the question of why we are alive, we must recover the vitality and authenticity of who we are in relationship to the circumstances in which we live. We have to dislodge the masks we developed as children and reclaim the soul-force that makes each of us unique and important in the whole web of life. Being seen and received as we *are* is an important invitation to authenticity, a chance to relax the armor that we usually wear against criticism and to be reassured by the presence of another person.

Even though our inborn qualities are part of our genetic makeup, we are influenced by those around us, called forth or squelched by the community in which we grow up or choose as adults. While heredity and environment are important because they shape our response to the spiritual realm, they are limited to the *chronos* world of time and space. If we are to reclaim our connection with the *kairos* realm of spirit, we need other mirrors.

Mirroring is a sacred skill that lets us see who we are rather than what someone else wants us to be. Like a match to tinder, feelings flame brightly when someone touches the true self. Having someone to mirror our gifts is not something we can earn or control. Such persons seem to arrive when we most need them (could they be angels in disguise?), even though we have tried to institutionalize those relationships with mentoring programs, therapy, and even spiritual direction.

Exposure to people who model a life of call is an important part of building language and awareness of call. Every community contains such people, though they may be difficult to find because they do not seek attention. They are the "unsung heroes" who keep a local community vital with their service, whether that be commercial, educational, or artistic. In her book *The Eighth Day of Creation*, Elizabeth O'Connor described such a mirroring person as a "patron of gifts," someone who sees, names, and nourishes the seeds of who we truly are.[3]

In the years during which my husband went to Vietnam, a local potter, Louis Mideke, invited me to use his studio in the evenings. "I'm in the house if you have any questions," he told me after showing me the rudimentary skills I would need. I would come each evening after a day of teaching junior high school, switch on the lights in the warm little studio, and work in the stillness. On Saturdays, we would open the kiln, holding up the warm pots like jeweled eggs in the frosty air. Each week, this was a celebration of our creativity. Louis might comment, "I see you've smoothed that handle joint. I was meaning to say something . . . ," so I knew he was watching but with kindly eyes. Never critical, he let me grow at my own speed. He let me know it was safe to ask questions, to make mistakes, to learn my own way. He mirrored my creativity and called forth dormant interests that would later develop in my professional work. Through clay, I reclaimed the joy of learning my own way.[4]

Clay also took me back to the earth where my sense of God was expanded even further. As I worked with the clay and read of the Southwest Indian traditions associated with handbuilt forms I admired, my soul resonated with their traditional tales of humans birthed from the earth, who reverenced sky and wind as the presence of Spirit. I began to notice metaphors of clay and potter in the Bible as well, letting my hands take me to the strong images of God as mountain and wind, fire and voice in the Psalms. Clay helped to reconnect me with Scripture in an experiential Hebrew way, as opposed to the Greek separation of body and spirit I had learned in church. In the pottery studio, the mystic in me stirred after long years of abstraction, reclaiming a child's way of knowing through my body sensibilities.

• *HERO & HEARTHKEEPER* •

In his book *Hero with a Thousand Faces*, Joseph Campbell wrote of the "heroic monomyth" that pervades the myths of all cultures.[5] The hero's journey mirrors the life quest each one of us undertakes to discover our true identity—the unfolding of call or "soul's code." In the mythic tradition, the Hero is often an orphan who has been cared for by foster parents. He sets off in search of his true identity, while the Hearthkeeper stays behind, holding the space for his return. She maintains their holy bond by drawing out secret gifts with wit and perception rather than weapons.

Campbell cites Homer's eighth century B.C. epic of Odysseus and Penelope as the quintessential example of Hero and Hearthkeeper. Odysseus leaves home as an arrogant, egocentric warrior. He masks his true identity to get through many trials and traps, and he lives out the three-part heroic journey that Campbell describes as separation, initiation, and return. (These are similar to William Bridges' cycle of transition: endings, neutrality, and beginnings—see Chapter 1, page 22). This first phase, separation, roughly parallels the first two stages of the soulwork cycle and requires leave-taking, loss, and loneliness.

While Odysseus breaks through the bondage of resistance, faces adversity, and undertakes a dangerous and unknown path, Penelope lives out the Hearthkeeper archetype, caring for their son and fending off suitors who try to persuade her that Odysseus will never return. She remains faithful to her marriage vows and grows progressively more wily and clever at protecting what she values most. If the Hero's journey is external and full of physical challenges, the Hearthkeeper's journey is mainly internal, marked by loyalty to what she loves and perceptive skills to identify help when it comes.

When Odysseus finally returns to Penelope, he has discovered the richness and compassion associated with home and care, while Penelope has developed her disciplined warrior skills. Their separation was essential for each of them to reclaim parts of themselves. Yet Campbell also notes that it is during separation that unexpected helpers arrive when they are needed, not to rescue but to guide.

In a nice gender reversal of the typical pattern, Gideon personifies the Hearthkeeper, and Esther, the Hero archetype. Each of the helpers they encountered during the separation phase mirrored the strengths that would be needed for the journey ahead. Gideon's response to his mysterious helper, the angel, was that of the hospitable Hearthkeeper: "Wait here, while I prepare some food for you." Loyalty and tradition aided Gideon in his effort to test the angel's reliability. Waiting created space in the narrative for something else to happen.

As a classic Hero figure, Esther left home unconsciously, thrust out of her culture and into the court by her beauty—and her cousin's ambitions. In the separation phase, Mordecai swore her to secrecy about her Jewish heritage, so Esther became self-contained, solitary, a spiritually-armored warrior in a hostile environment. Her helper was Hegai, the eunuch who coached her in a year of preparation before she was named Queen. To move on to the initiation phase, she needed to find her heroic core in order to function outside of the traditional rules that bound women to a subservient role in the court.

Whether Hero or Hearthkeeper, we must find those helpers who can mirror essential strengths and remind us of the larger story to which we belong.

• *WITNESS & WAITING* •

Something in us knows that call will separate us from the herd, take us away from what we know, away from others who shape our reality for us. The loneliness of claiming call can be assuaged by the presence of a witness, often a stranger who lives outside our normal circles of friendship or work. Although the basic form of who we are meant to be is inborn, it usually takes someone to draw it out and give us language for what is possible. Reclaiming is not simply a process of reminiscence but of observation and action. This is where a coach, mentor, spiritual director, or therapist can help. A witness validates our truth and confirms our body-knowing.

One characteristic of a witness is the ability to wait, to simply be present. When I was in high school, I got up in a cold, dark house to practice the piano every morning at six A.M. Shortly after I would sit down to play, my father would be in the kitchen, making coffee and putting on the oatmeal. Then he would settle down on the couch with his medical reading to keep me company. He never corrected my playing or appeared to pay the slightest attention to what I was doing, but he was there, waiting with me while I gave myself to the music. Even though it had been thirty years since those early morning practice hours, my father's death left me lonely on the planet until I could begin to reclaim the power of music and his presence in other ways—by singing, working outdoors, and participating in liturgy. In telling this story to the therapist who served as my witness, I could remember and reclaim how important my father's waiting had been.

Reclaiming parts of our past means having a place to tell hidden parts of our story, to remember secrets of past survival. Both therapy and religious ritual can help us recall and reconnect with our strengths. I believe the physical involvement is essential for healing precognitive adaptation. Bodywork is a form of therapy particularly suited to this stage because it combines touch and words. Rosen bodywork has provided me with an experience of being met at the places of inarticulate holding in my body—barriers that kept me from hearing the call embedded in my very cells. Begun by Marion Rosen, a German physical therapist who moved to this country before World War II, Rosen noticed small cues in breathing and body tension that she "coached" verbally and with touch, developing a safe space between herself and the client.[6] My experience of this bodywork feels like untangling yarn that has been twisted or knotted for years. Oddly enough, taking communion, or Eucharist, has the same effect for me, for much the same reason: It is a body experience of witness and waiting.

An effective witness waits while we reclaim what we need from the past. When the angel appeared in his story, Gideon, like many of us, did not trust the divine nature of his angelic visitor. He was willing to offer hospitality, but he was suspicious of the angel's grandiose message from God to become a "mighty warrior." And he discounted God's pledge of partnership. When the angel replied, "I will wait," it was a stunning response! Is it possible that God is waiting for us to see that we are *already* connected with the divine realm? For us to hear our call as an invitation to relationship with the *kairos* realm of timelessness? For us to recognize that "call" does not take a special ritual, academic degrees, or even moral purity? Biblical stories suggest that Spirit comes to all kinds of people, particularly the lost, the least, and the lonely. And when we are not ready, angels wait. God has all the time in the universe. It is we who are caught in the anxiety of time and finitude.

Finding a witness may mean finding social structures to hold the vague or specific fears that a new call can create. The reclaiming stage of call is often a slow process because we do not know the stories of family and religious tradition, so to reclaim our strength from the past may mean naming things for the first time. Instead, we watch TV news, entertainment, and sports that are devoid of the archetypal dramas that can help us understand deeper currents at work in our lives. Instead of developing contact with sacred images, we speed through things as though accumulating the greatest number of experiences would make us winners in the game of life. Having some kind of small group, particularly one within a worshipping community, can provide a container for the fears we can barely articulate, reflecting back the kernel of truth we cannot see for ourselves.

Having a group that will bear witness to the sacred elements of daily experience is an important way to reclaim lost parts of our lives. In my weekly mission group at Seekers, I have the opportunity to share a written report with my spiritual director and talk with a group about where God is present in my life. Following guidelines that prevent comment and "cross-talk" about our sharing, over time this group has become a safe place to offer the tender edges of a new call. Having a safe place to be a beginner is one important element of reclaiming resources for the call that is becoming visible in this second stage.

• MUSIC & STORY •

Gathering courage to embrace a new call is a process of learning, of drawing on the past by reexamining personal experience, family traditions, religious training, and cultural myths. Not only do we need to reclaim parts of our personal history, but we also need to confront cultural power systems designed to keep us in place. Our larger work is to reclaim a fresh image of God, to reconnect with sacred story of *kairos* reality.

Reclaiming God's presence can happen in many ways beyond the traditional methods of sacraments, prayer, and scripture. When we are facing a transition that touches fears about our very existence, we naturally turn to music and story for inspiration and encouragement. They help us "re-member" our scattered community, energize the people involved, and reconnect us with a larger vision for the work we are called to do.

In a radio interview on the anniversary of Martin Luther King, Jr.'s death, his wife, Coretta Scott King, told how singing together had helped people gather their courage for confrontations with the police during the Civil Rights Movement. "Music was always part of the movement," she said, "It made us feel strong. It connected us. When you're singing with a large group of people, it lifts you up—gives you a sense of power." [7] Out of the traditions of Black gospel music and singing the blues, the Civil Rights Movement claimed the moral authority to change the system of American apartheid. By the time Martin Luther King, Jr. gave his "I Have a Dream" speech in 1963, his dream of a better world was shared by many, Black and White. The movement reclaimed the power of God's dream for a more just and merciful society, and music gave them access to that collective presence.

Music has the capacity to move body and soul, joining us with realms beyond thought and plan. Not only can music "lift you up," but it can heal, soothe, and satisfy unspoken longings. As a musical instrument, the human voice is always with us, ready with speech and song to inspire hope, call forth courage for common effort. Cadence, rhythm, and sound invite us to dance, to move and bless in religious ritual, and also to blend our energies together in physical labor—a natural way to reclaim our sense of connection with others. Music and story take us beyond ourselves, into the realm of spirit and community.

Music was probably my first spiritual practice, giving me regular contact with the spiritual realm of passion and beauty. Reminiscent of my teenage early morning piano practice, I still use the word "practice" to describe the regular morning habits that I do to stay in touch with the realm of God, to restore a sense of belonging to something larger and more complex than my self and our culture. A spiritual practice need not be complicated, but it does need to be regular. It is a reminder of relationship with all things. Just as I stretched my hands with scales and chords before turning to the music I would learn as a teenager, I now stretch my soul with regular practice of sitting in silence, noticing the images of my inner geography, keeping a journal, and walking. My practice also includes regular times of singing with a chant group, where we experiment with improvised chanting. When we gather, I am most aware of our *being* together. We reconnect with life and breath and sound, witnessing Spirit in each other.

When we are faced with change at the soul level, we also turn to heroic stories for inspiration and encouragement. The biblical story of Moses leading his people out from Egypt is one we return to in every generation. Joseph Campbell has made "the heroic quest" part of our common knowledge about the soul's journey. George Lucas put it on large screen with his "Star Wars" trilogy, and Clarissa Pinkola Estes filled in the gender gap with *Women Who Run With the Wolves.* In all these stories, the hero or heroine hears a call (or is forced into a quest) and must move toward wisdom through a series of obstacles and trials. In the biblical story of Esther, she had to rely on her memory of childhood stories to reclaim the power of her relationship with God. When she first entered the King's harem, it was not safe for her to identify her Jewish heritage. She eventually had to reconnect with the Exodus stories of God's faithfulness and power before she was ready to act.

We, too, turn to stories to reconnect us with meaning and purpose. In the early sixties, while others were beginning to demonstrate against Vietnam and for civil rights, I was living in Alaska, struggling to understand why military force was sometimes needed. My husband, Peter, and I were a stereotypical couple, Hero and Hearthkeeper, on the outside, at least. As a Hearthkeeper, my negative feelings about using force were mostly personal. As a female, I had been taught not to fight; as an intellectual, I believed in rational discussion; as a Christian, I believed violence was wrong. I grew up with a strong antipathy for war. It seemed like a cosmic joke that I had married a man with an ROTC commitment to serve.

After we had been married less than a month, Peter went to the field for thirty days, and I was stuck in a one-room apartment in Fairbanks at twenty below zero, with no friends, no phone, and no car. First, I got sick, which is often the Hearthkeeper's spiritual battlefield. Then I realized that no one would find me if I died (oh yes, I was feeling that dramatically awful). So I dragged myself out of bed and went to the local library where it was warm and there were books to read, hundreds of them. Soon I found myself immersed in thick novels about the Holocaust, intuitively reaching for help to explain why force was sometimes needed. Remembering the Jewish Holocaust gave me some perspective on the purpose and meaning of what Peter was doing in the Army.

Stories continued to help me reclaim rejected parts of my life. My love for Bible stories as heroic drama was rekindled by my experience with clay in the sixties and expanded by Faith At Work in the seventies. But by the mid-seventies, I had become acutely aware of the patriarchal bias in the biblical record and church structures, and I began looking for ways to reclaim my heritage rather than leaving it altogether. What I needed was a conceptual framework that would help me interpret my life and the world around me from a biblical perspective that did not leave my identity as a woman out of the picture.

I began to understand the Hebrew word for "heart" through my experience with Faith At Work, and that gave me a conceptual framework to break through the separation of body and spirit, and reclaim my soul. Not only is "heart" used to describe Hearthkeeper's realm of emotions and spirituality, but "heart" also includes the heroic qualities of willpower, ethical discernment, physical and spiritual maturity, as in the great commandments "to love God with heart, soul, mind and strength and your neighbor as yourself."[8] The idea of including emotions and physical experience in religious life was new to me, and I found it both frightening and exciting. Relational theology gave me a way to join the powerful feelings of physical energy, sexuality, and spirituality on behalf of call. I could see the radical way that Jesus included women, even though their stories in the Bible were short and often truncated. As my understanding of God began to expand, I was able to reclaim some of the goodness of my own religious heritage and stay in the church at a time when many women felt they had to leave. The music and stories of faith continued to nourish my soul toward the call I felt as a potter.

• *BETWEEN STORIES* •

Since the mid-sixties, our culture has let go of old certainties and not come to a common world view. As Walter Wink says in *The Powers That Be*, we have split heaven and earth into separate spheres and lost a sense of the whole.[9] As some say, we are living in a time "between stories."

While we may be living between stories, we are not without images that may yet bring us the language of Oneness mystics have always been able to see. We know that images precede language and when images are shared in community, language will not be far behind. On retreats that I lead, when I ask people for images of their spiritual life, they usually include an image of suffering and an image of hope. Most often the suffering shows some human-created condition of war or isolation—what may be our modern acknowledgment of sin. The sign of hope is nearly always a relationship of tenderness or vulnerability or newness, frequently involving a child. Intuitively, we long for that kind of innocent connection and caring. These images speak of what we know at a soul level—that we live in an imperfect world and often choose harm rather than harmony. They also show that we share a common hope that love will find a way to recapture the sense of reciprocity and connection that flows through the sacred stories of many cultures.

Over and over again, I see signs of a new cosmic story breaking into language. When I ask people to "make a collage of your beliefs and include some image of Spirit," almost always people choose a picture from interstellar space or from cellular biology, the outer and inner structures of creation. No longer do they reach for personal images, such as Michelangelo's famous image of an old bearded male reaching out to touch the extended finger of a young male from the "Creation" painting on the Sistine Chapel ceiling, even though I am careful to provide those options. Instead, they pick startling photos from *Scientific American, Science* or *Technology Review* of the unfolding wonder of creation. These pictures of the larger, dynamic universe speak to people of God's true nature. Although many still pray to "Our Father, who art in heaven . . . ," the image of God we are holding is moving beyond space and time into mystery, into wonder.

In many ways, what we are replacing is not the traditional Christian story but the images provided by Renaissance and Enlightenment painters who were the first to put man at the apex of creation, with women and children somewhere below. As modern science opens the universe to us, we are in the process of shifting from a Newtonian worldview to a relational worldview in which humans are an important part of an organic whole, but not the sole focus of the creation story. The mutuality and interactivity of all matter provides new space for a variety of human relationships and new visions of functional cooperation rather than permanent institutions. The shift from a mechanical model of the universe to the quantum world of relationships resonates with soul!

• *A RELATIONAL PERSPECTIVE* •

A relational perspective helps us reclaim the notion of call for everyone. The overall biblical story provides language for increasing consciousness of our relationship with one another and with creation—the original meaning of keeping the Sabbath. Rather than living "between stories," perhaps we are living between worldviews. A static worldview seeks "right answers" from the Bible, while a relational worldview means that biblical stories provide images and metaphors for the great mysteries of human life—creativity, love, forgiveness, evil, pain, and death—in the context of creation itself. When we come to the biblical story with the understanding that creation is still in the process of forming and dissolving, call takes on new importance.

Bill Moyers guided a popular television discussion series on the biblical stories of Genesis. Rather than seeking a particular interpretation or truth, Moyers set the stage for dialogue by bringing a number of people together from different theological perspectives. The format itself was relational. One of the participants, Roberta Hestenes, spoke about the question of work and call this way:

> . . . work itself is a gift. It's a calling. We live in a culture that says not to work is the big ideal. Retire early. Have a vacation. Figure out energetically how not to work. Here in the Garden (of Eden) we see that work is part of what it means to be human. Work is the co-creation of beauty and order and fruitfulness.[10]

The participants in this series brought many different perspectives to the ancient Genesis story. Even as they debated, discovered differences, and came to new insights, viewers had the opportunity to try on different interpretations and come to their own conclusions. Moyers and his panel helped modern viewers reclaim the biblical story as a dynamic matrix for individual call.

• *BEYOND RECLAIM* •

Joining a small group or ongoing community that has a spiritual consciousness is a good way to find a mirror for our deeper gifts. Making space for retreat with others who share our search for call can provide additional resources for reclaiming a context for call. Any church service, through story, song, and prayer, will include celebration of deeper rhythms of death and rebirth.

Eventually, however, the question of call moves beyond personal healing and remembering the past. As we allow the images and stories of others to inform and inspire our action, we begin to gather energy around our new call. As we reclaim our tribe and traditions, we begin to put our individual concerns in a larger context and discover a sense of God's perspective as well as our own. As our community helps us reclaim both personal and collective memories, we catch a glimmer of additional meaning for the call in us that is beginning to emerge in believable form. What we reclaim from our past can lead us toward Stage Three, Revelation.

Here is an exercise that I have found to be helpful in this transition. You may want to try it with a group or on your own:

If you are in a group, stand in a circle and start the exercise here:
- Be aware of the circle of people you are standing with this moment.
- Look at them carefully. Notice their differences and register God's intentionality in that.

If you are by yourself, you can start the exercise here:
- Now imagine your mother standing behind you, having given birth to you.
- And her mother behind her . . . and so on, back as far as your mind can stretch.
- Notice where you shift from personal memory to stories you have heard.

- Then notice where you shift from family stories to ethnic or national identity.
- And finally, notice where you shift from history to religious tradition.
- Be aware of the voices from your past that now echo in your heart . . .
- Because only you, alive in this day and age, have the power to make changes.

Stage Three: REVELATION

CHAPTER 5

Flaming tongues licked the night air from every hole in the garbage can that served as our temporary kiln. We drew close to the fire, staring silently at the consuming flames or talking quietly in pairs. It felt like holy ground.

The next day we pulled small black pots from the filmy ash, exclaiming over each one, noticing the iridescent blush where the fire had kissed a shoulder here, a rim there. Finally I drew out a tiny basket, and we saw it was cupped around a perfect white pearl of clay.

"Gayle's baby!" one woman exclaimed. "That's my prayer icon."

We stood amazed. Gayle had been on the list to come to this year's weekend retreat on "soulmaking" at Kirkridge. She had come every year. When I arrived at Kirkridge to lead the retreat, a call from her pastor had been waiting. Gayle had died that day in premature childbirth, but her baby was still alive.

Because we had expected Gayle to be on retreat with us, I shared her story with the group. After years of trying to have a child, Gayle and her husband had adopted two children. And now we were holding her new baby in our prayers.

The white pearl of clay nestled in its blackened nest seemed to be a sign. There was no logical explanation for why the smoky fire left this one small piece untouched.

Several years later, I heard that Gayle's daughter was thriving. I do not remember why the maker of that prayer icon had felt so connected to those events, but I knew we had glimpsed the mystery of death and life in the fire's choice.

If Stage Two is set in community and past tradition, then Stage Three opens the future like the night sky full of stars. In this third stage some event or insight draws the curtain back, for an instant, between temporal and eternal reality, between *chronos* and *kairos* time. We glimpse another dimension where possibility abounds and fear is, for the moment, overtaken. We are transported into another realism. Stars fall, a rainbow appears, a bush burns without being consumed . . . a pearl of clay survives as a sign of new life. The future opens, and suddenly we feel the euphoria of Eden if only for the moment. Everything is connected, and we sense the whole, feel the fusion of a timeless realm. Ecstatic. Pulsing with life, we touch the vital core. And then . . . and then . . . the curtain closes again. We are left to struggle with bringing the vision to birth in time and space. We vacillate, at one moment feeling ready to move ahead and then back off, wondering, "Is this call? Shall I move forward with this impulse?"

In this third stage of call, we have the opportunity to say "yes" to the unseen world. By stepping into a *kairos* moment, we can see the whole from a divine perspective. We also have the power to say "no," to deny what we have seen and stay with the old ways. Stage Three is a struggle between caution and custom, between what we "know" and a brief glimpse of something larger than ourselves. It is

Stage 3: Revelation

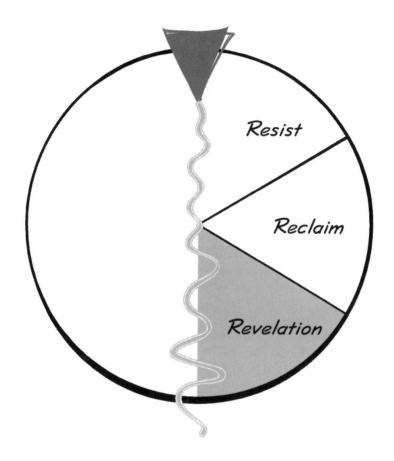

a transitional stage, full of ambivalence and uncertainty, possibility and potential dangers. That is the way new vision is born into the world.

There is a difference, however, between a moment of ecstasy, of inspiration or insight and a *kairos* moment of revelation, but it may be difficult to tell the difference when it is happening. A young friend, familiar with the language of call and uncertain of her career goals, returned from a "semester at sea" convinced that she was being called to India: "The children are so beautiful, the colors so vibrant, the air charged with spirituality . . . I think I'm being called to go there, though I don't really know what I would do." She was ready to consider her experience a revelation, but she knew that the thrill of beauty or ecstasy was not enough to draw out the effort it would take to prepare for work in India. Her uncertainty is typical of this stage.

If we have no mythic vocabulary, no framework for interpretation, we may isolate this "glimpse of heaven." We may see it as a product of our imagination—and perhaps gather an artifact to remind ourselves that we have had a "sacred" moment—but not be able to integrate what we have seen. A spiritual high does not necessarily reveal God's sacred purpose nor does it automatically lead to action. As long as we continue to separate body from spirit, we will not be able to experience revelation as guidance and enter into an ongoing relationship with that divine presence. The step from imagination to revelation is a small but critical one in the soul's journey.

• CONTEXT •

As children, we believe in magic: miraculous rescues, enchanted animals, special objects. "Growing up" means learning the boundaries between wishing and reality and, eventually, "putting away childish things." As adults, we may want to believe and yet cannot. We live in a culture that undermines faith with an artificial distinction among science and art and faith. We compare and contrast, criticize and compete, set one against another in a digital world of on/off, up/down, in/out. We lapse into the "littleness" of personal idiosyncrasies, mocking those who would call us to something better, something bigger. If we hear voices, we assume it must be pathological. We are living with the grave consequences of a crumbling belief system and have not yet developed a broader, more inclusive cosmology that connects rather than excludes.

Because we have no common story to interpret these *kairos* events, we may have revealing moments that are a form of discovery but do not suggest Spirit or a call to the soul. We may have wonderful, serendipitous meetings that offer no particular guidance or direction, suggest no meaning for a larger purpose. We may believe in revelation but keep it personal and private, short-circuiting the role of revelation in shaping call. Or we may keep such "sightings" silent because we do not want to explore the consequences.

Surging interest in all forms of spirituality suggests that our hunger for belief is still strong, despite the efforts of scientific rationality to discredit the realm of Spirit. Spiritual experiences can be odd occurrences, spooky and disorienting—especially without a context of belief and tradition or without belief in a power greater than ourselves. One reason to work with biblical stories of call is to build an interpretive context for extraordinary events. Both Jewish and Christian scriptures are ripe with these revelatory moments: a bush burns and is not consumed, a voice comes out of a cloud, waters part and then close again on pursuing enemies, a star guides three astrologers to a stable in Bethlehem. These archetypal stories of biblical faith expand moments of spiritual insight beyond personal rescue and reveal the presence of God who is making some effort to communicate with us. These stories illustrate a basic premise of faith—that our consciousness is connected with a divine source.

The biblical tradition of call can provide a context for miraculous events that happen to all of us. If we have a framework for understanding the dynamics of call, then we can suspend our disbelief when revelation pulls the curtain back on another realm. Heroic myth and sacred story can reveal a deeper truth than we are conscious of. They can provide a context for isolated incidents to become part of the fabric of call. If we are living out of "soul consciousness," expecting *kairos* moments of revelation, call looms momentarily large. Time and space dissolve. We see the whole, the essence, if only for a moment. We touch the Divine in what Jung called a *numinous* experience and Quakers call "way opening."

• *SIGNS* •

Stage Three is full of signs and wonders that suggest there is another world we cannot quite see. Mystery and strange encounters intrigue us, sometimes drawing us to bizarre explanations. We notice when serendipities occur and odd coincidences happen. Something signals that another dimension of guidance is breaking into everyday reality. Weird connections catch our attention, make us sniff the wind for miracles. A word "hits home" in our gut, or the same song keeps recurring in different places. An encounter brings a deep emotional response and suddenly the gates of heaven open.

What Jung called *synchronicity* often occurs in the third stage, when we are looking for hints of divine presence. The right person calls, a door opens, somebody gives us just what we need. Miracles happen. Synchronicity is something we cannot explain with logic and probability. It is a sign that something else is at work. I remember the time I was sitting in the middle of a sales meeting, hearing this incredible story from a man who kept saying, *"I don't know why I'm telling you this, but . . . "*

> *I was driving on a particularly desolate road in Alberta, tired, angry, and drunk. I don't remember what happened, but there was a terrible accident. Incredibly, there was an empty ambulance going the other way. They stopped and scraped me up off the road—both legs broken, all my ribs broken, lungs collapsed, heart stopped.*
>
> *The medic shocked me awake and held up a picture in my wallet, asking me, "Who is this?"*
>
> *"My daughter," I tried to say.*
>
> *"Go back to sleep. She has a message for you."*
>
> *I drifted off and there she was: eight years old, saying "Dad, I love you."*
>
> *I knew I had to make the effort—go back to my body—stay alive.*

The miracle was the ambulance. What are the chances the ambulance would have been there?

Then later he added: *Ah. I know why I told you that story. Tomorrow I fly home for the holidays, to be near my former wife and daughter. I needed to remember why I'm still here. I missed my AA meeting this morning. God must have sent you to listen. Thanks.*

For this man, not only was the ambulance a sign of divine protection, but having listeners who encouraged his "story" was a sign that he was not alone as he tried to rebuild his life, stay off drugs, and reclaim connections with his family. He was an exile, far from home, but not abandoned. This is the work of revelation, to reclaim our connections with the unseen realm of divine mystery that quickens life and calls to us like wild geese at dusk.

• *BREAKTHROUGH* •

Sacred scriptures in all traditions include signs and symbols that point to the realm of Spirit.

Sometimes the scrim between "now" and "not yet" opens when something shocks us. When Gideon left the angel to go and prepare some food, he had no intention of heeding the call to leave his winepress for a warrior's path. When he returned, he was in for a surprise. The angel told him to put his meat and bread on a rock, and when the angel touched the meat with his staff, fire flared from the rock. Gideon's offering was consumed in a dramatic revelation. It became a burnt offering, and suddenly he knew he was in the presence of the Holy. Terrified, Gideon cried out, "Alas, I have seen the angel of the Lord face to face!" He fully expected to die!

In Esther's story, Mordecai's prophetic word lifted the veil of mystery for her: "Who knows, but that you were born for such a time as this." Mordecai held Esther's destiny up and gave it a name. He took on a priestly role, mediating the sacred for her. Being able to recognize a greater purpose for the situation we are in can give us hope and strength to do what needs to be done, as it did for Esther. It can also fill us with terror because we glimpse the enormity of the task and the impossibility of doing it by ourselves, as was the case for Gideon.

When we have a tradition that can name moments of revelation as part of God's pattern of communication, we may be able to understand them as part of God's call. At The Church of the Saviour, where the language of call has been a guiding principle for more than fifty years, members expect such breakthrough moments and seek them when a new call might be emerging. Gordon Cosby speaks of call as simple, impossible, and persistent. Simple, because it fits with God's purpose for the world: feed the hungry, clothe the naked, shelter the children. Impossible, because it is too big, too complex for one person to accomplish alone. And persistent, because God has planted this seed of purpose and will not be discouraged by our unwillingness to say "yes."[1]

However it comes, revelation means seeing the whole picture. Like Gideon, we may suddenly find ourselves in the presence of God, called to a work we never expected, filled with the fire of Spirit. Like Esther, we may understand there will be consequences if we fail to act. On a small scale, I often encourage people to notice their body response to people, situations, or stories. Revelation can be a simple feeling of a "rightness" or fit, a kind of body-knowing—perhaps tears that rise unexpectedly or persistent dreams. Sometimes we simply know it is time to put our resistance aside and say "yes" to the unknown path ahead.

• LOVER & SEEKER •

In Stage Three the opposing archetypes of Lover and Seeker both contain the possibility of revelation. In this stage of call, we come to what Joseph Campbell called "the initiation phase,"[2] full of trials and tests, serendipitous events and strange tasks that reveal the heretofore unknown dimensions of call.

Lover and Seeker, as Carol Pearson describes them,[3] each respond to revelation differently. The Lover connects from the heart, sensing universal truth from within. The Seeker listens and watches for external clues. Both are drawn forward by what is revealed in moments of clarity and both incorporate revelation to sustain their call through times of confusion and diversion.

Typical of the Lover, Esther felt hesitation and ambivalence about her call. The Lover listens internally for heartbeat sounds, for dreams and intuitions about the next steps. The Lover will be drawn to people and places where s/he can proceed by including, accepting, and affirming the new, even if there is risk involved. Esther had to stay in a hostile environment and use her fear as radar for daring action, strict boundaries, discernment, and exquisite timing. For us, as for Esther, revelation may mean digging deeper for qualities of courage and discernment to find a way through a situation that cannot be changed.

In modern life, Lover energies are mostly marginalized or repressed because of the emotional entanglements involved. Because the body sensation of revelation is the same as falling in love, Stage Three frequently begins with infatuation, particularly among those of the Buster and Boomer generations who are wrestling with the questions of "Who am I?" or "What is my work?" We "fall in love" with the qualities in someone else that we are meant to embrace for an expanded sense of self. Although not often acknowledged, fixing our attention on someone who embodies a piece of what we are being called to is a common way for call to become visible. We may even feel "possessed" by something other than ourselves. As we are struggling to shrug off a persona shaped for the ego needs of others, falling in love with someone who is not appropriate or who is "forbidden" is a strange way that revelation often comes.

John Sanford, in his classic book *The Invisible Partners,* describes the dynamic energy of projection that occurs when we "fall in love" or "fall in hate" with someone.[4] One sign that we are projecting an unborn part of ourselves onto someone else is that "falling in love" happens quickly and feels obsessive. If we begin to understand the archetypal energy behind an obsessive attraction, we have some choices about how to incorporate and direct that energy.

The danger, at this stage, is making the Lover archetype literal. Popular culture condones sexuality without addressing the possibility of spiritual growth in such attraction. We can end up trapped in a never-ending cycle of hope and disappointment, not realizing that we have the power to take our lives in our own hands, that infatuation might provide clues to call.

The Seeker, on the other hand, is ready to leave all behind, venture outward with no baggage, dismiss what has been held so dear. Some people need to leave the past behind, even destroy symbols of the past to proceed. We need the energy and willingness of the Seeker to move forward into the future, to unmask hidden elements that have kept us mired in the past, and to break up the journey into smaller manageable segments.

Gideon did not claim his Seeker path easily or willingly. "My clan is the weakest and I am the least of my tribe," he told the angel. In Stage Two, Gideon clung to his traditional ways by offering hospitality, but revelation came when flame sprang from the stone and burned up his offering. This startling event cracked open his shell of tradition, convincing Gideon to leave his old ways behind and follow God's call.

True revelation demands a response. The angel directed Gideon to tear down his father's altar and build a new one to Yahweh with the same stones, then ordered him to sacrifice one of his father's cattle. The ancient practice of offering a sacrifice to mark a revelation may seem odd until we notice our willingness to sacrifice money and time to a therapist in exchange for help interpreting such revelatory events.

This act launched the Seeker in Gideon. Once he had claimed his allegiance to God, he could not go back. He had to destroy his father's place of worship and replace it with a sign of his new allegiance—to his own destiny. It was the internal preparation for Gideon to a more public phase of claiming God's call.

Gideon named his new altar "Peace," even though its immediate result was violence when a lynch mob formed to hunt for the culprit who destroyed Baal's altar. The new altar and its name give us a glimpse of the final outcome, of the revelation completed. Miraculously, Gideon's father gave him protection from the mob that demanded retribution for the destruction. "If Baal is angry, let Baal punish Gideon," his father said, siding with his son. Perhaps Gideon's courage also freed his father to reclaim a forgotten faithfulness to God.

Revelation as a step toward claiming call requires both Lover and Seeker energy. Individually, we would probably prefer either the Lover role or the Seeker role over the other, but soulwork requires both. Love without search is sentimental and often stifling. The Lover tends to hang on too long, to sacrifice and give up self for what has been—as Esther was tempted to do. Search without love feels rootless and disconnected. The Seeker looks for novelty, for newness—as Gideon was ready to do. Often exhausted, the Seeker does not allow space and time to gather energy for the crossing ahead. But in concert, Seeker and Lover develop discernment and courage to act.

• BREAKING THE BARRIER OF FEAR •

When God's intent is revealed, we, like Gideon and Esther, have to make a decision. There is usually something "sacred" from our family or ego structure that stands in the way of responding to God's call. It must be dismantled or left behind—an idol smashed, an addiction faced, a paralyzing fear overcome. Some "father's altar" must be torn down. At every stage of call, we can say "no." We can choose to leave our "father's altar" standing, to live in fear because we have not claimed the fullness of who we are created to be.

Biblical stories do not deny the fear of dismantling our "father's altar" to follow God's new call. As though to underscore the importance of call, biblical angels often announce their presence with the disquieting words, "Fear not!" They recognize our fear when a new call comes even if we do not. We always have the choice to turn down that invitation. Or we can choose to take action to break through our barrier of fear.

A decision to act means entertaining the possibility that God can reveal something entirely out of character. It means putting a partial vision into action, taking a small (or large) step on the basis of this new understanding. Often we need help to get through this stage because transformation is not really self-directed. Revelation requires that we see things in their larger context of mystery and challenge. Stage Three is the time to "leave home," to separate from unconscious patterns and claim an independent vision —even when that feels as if we are choosing death instead of the safety and comfort of known ways. Our action requires us to act on what is revealed rather than what we have known.

Because the stakes are so high at this point of the cycle, we may also find ourselves repeating all the dysfunctional and non-productive behavior of earlier stages. At a body level, we may test the source of call, asking if there is indeed a reality beyond ourselves. We may engage in destructive behavior that can be a sign we are standing at the edge of decision, afraid to commit ourselves to the journey ahead. Our internal or unconscious ambivalence may be acted out in other arenas. We may take chances with driving, neglect preparation for an important meeting, forget appointments, fight with a spouse, or have an affair. Or we may come to the moment of commitment and back down, repeating the first three stages in a kind of "ungrounded" spirituality instead of crossing into action on the other side. Revelation is a time of danger and opportunity, yet failure to act can send us back to Stage One in a boring waltz of possibility that never gets embodied.

Revelation is also a time when we can seek discernment about how and when to act. In Stage Three, waiting is a way of nurturing the future. One way to participate consciously in waiting and revelation is to go on retreat. Step aside from the usual. Find a spiritual director. Take a "wellness day" in silence. Walk. Breathe. Journal. Do not fill up the time with something else. You may want a specific structure that involves body movement, a cleansing fast, some slow activity like fishing—anything that is a change of pace.

In Twelve-Step groups, making a "fearless and thorough moral inventory" of injuries we may have inflicted, as well as our strengths, is another way to process Stage Three. In more religious circles, doing a "spiritual autobiography" offers a way to sort through the past and discern the threads of call for the future. Writing such a narrative forces us to seek an organizing principle, something that will give form and shape to our story and help us recognize the thread of our call.

• *LISTENING* •

Seeking a revelation requires commitment to listening. Robert Greenleaf wrote about the role of listening to one another in his book *Servant Leadership*. As a way to hear the voice of God, he says we need to call forth the "prophetic word" by our attentiveness:

> The variable that marks some periods as barren and some as rich in prophetic vision is in the interest, the level of seeking, the responsiveness of the hearers. The variable is not in the presence or absence or the relative quality and force of the prophetic voices. Prophets grow in stature as people respond to their message. If their early attempts are ignored or spurned, their talent may wither away. It is seekers, then, who make prophets, and the initiative of any one of us in searching for and responding to the voice of contemporary prophets may mark the turning point in their growth and service.[5]

Greenleaf's perception is quite different from the prevailing notion that only leaders know what is good for the group. Although his book was published in the seventies, Greenleaf was speaking from his understanding of how God's call breaks into the lives of ordinary people. To acknowledge this extraordinary power of listening, The Seekers Church where I belong took its name from Greenleaf's words: "It is seekers, then, who make prophets."

In our busy and noisy culture, such listening is rare. We generally expect therapists and counselors to do it for a fee, but one of the beliefs of the Seekers community is that anyone who listens can be a healing presence for others. Over the years, we have found that our capacity for silence has increased in proportion to our capacity for listening, both individually and collectively. A young woman in my mission group wrote this description of how her practice of listening resulted in both parties having an experience of extraordinary revelation:

> *Leslie and I sat across from each other and started a conversation about her poetry and about my unemployment. But during the part when we were talking about the poetry, a strange thing happened. We were sitting in the middle of a long cafeteria table, and the place was very loud. People were talking and laughing all around us.*
>
> *Gradually, it was as if all the people around us melted together and faded away, and all the noise around us somehow melted together to form a kind of constant background hum. I could hear every word Leslie was saying, but it was as if I could hear her saying them with her heart as well as her voice, and as if I was hearing her with my heart as well as my ears.*
>
> *She had a question about her reaction to one of her best poems getting rejected by an important publisher. I recalled what she had shared with the group in a previous conference she had led, and I used that information to interpret her reaction. I have never before or since been involved so deeply, so intimately, in any discussion in my life. In that moment, I helped*

*her to answer her question but did it in a way that drew on
every single one of her gifts that I knew she had.*

*She just sat across the table from me and stared at me
with her mouth open. We forgot about our food, we forgot
about everything but what we were talking about. I felt in-
credibly joyful and connected. I felt full of potential and happiness and excitement. I had so much energy I was almost
bursting out of my chair, out of the room, out of the whole
building!* [6]

• *BEYOND REVELATION* •

In Stage Three, glimpses of the big picture are like a hologram in
which a small part reveals the whole. Impossible to absorb, a revelation can overwhelm or terrify us without a community or tradition to give it a context. Signs and wonders may serve only to amaze
or unhinge us, providing a spiritual "high" without any further results in the world. To claim the power of revelation for expanding
our sense of call, we need time and space for reflection. We may
also need an alternative language, such as music or art, that will
take us beyond the limits of linear thought into the realm of mystery and inspiration.

Accepting revelation implies that we are willing to be
changed, willing to be healed and expanded because we have
glimpsed a greater purpose for life. Story and myth suggest that
revelation expands our image of self, making space for new qualities and new possibilities. It is a period of being willing to give up
our defenses for the sake of call to the mystery of Spirit.

THE POISON RIVER

CHAPTER 6

Crossing the "poison river" is an image from my childhood, from a game my sister and I used to play endlessly on rainy days when we could not go outside. At my grandmother's house, the patterned borders where two rugs came together created a boundary that was too wide to jump across. Something frightening or evil lay there in our imagination. Our game was to contrive some artifice—bridge, boat, magic scarf, someone—to get us across this "poison river" between the rugs that seemed safe.

There is a truth in our childhood game of "poison river" that I am only beginning to appreciate. As adults, when we come to a barrier between belief and embodiment, we must confront our fears of radical change, of making a terrible mistake with the time we have, and challenge our fears of death. Call requires crossing. The Poison River is a dividing line between inspiration and application, separating affect from effect, keeping the feelings of love and body-connection in the private sphere away from the public sphere of institutions. Commitment is required to cross over into another way of being in the world. At the edge of the Poison River, it is possible to believe something wholeheartedly . . . and still not do it.

The Poison River flows from the mouth of call, tumbling down rapids, cascading over falls, creating a testing place for the soul to cross from private, individual experience to public, communal life. Many stay on the side of resist, reclaim, and revelation, never moving farther than the glimpses of God or special angelic interventions in Stage Three. We separate personal inner life from public outer expression. When that happens, we live bifurcated lives, functioning more as "human doings" in the public realm, wondering why we have lost our moral compass. We refuse to believe humans have the power to bring the Divine into flesh, and we do not bring the power of Spirit into public life. We set ourselves up for anxiety and addiction because we have forgotten that we are created for wholeness and relationship—with God, with ourselves, and with others.

If soul development is limited to the personal realm of feeling and spiritual highs, then increasing separation develops between personal beliefs and public actions, creating the kind of moral wasteland that we see today. Our "doing" and "being" stay separate. The cost of this split between our spiritual and physical lives is often nothing less than a loss of self.

• DECIDING •

There comes a time in each soulwork cycle when we need to make a commitment to take our call seriously, to take the plunge without knowing the outcome. Even if we have come to believe in the call and the caller, we still have to make a decision to *do* something about it. We have to decide whether to proceed or turn back. Finding a way to enter the terrifying waters of the unknown is crucial.

This river, which runs through ancient myths from every culture, signals that the barriers to a spiritually integrated life are real and that the requirements for living out one's call, instead of living out of habit, demand effort and risk. The image of a "poisoned river" is one that we know all too well. We have seen, literally, how toxic poisoning by unconscious or deliberate dumping of wastes can change what began as a clear and life-giving stream into a cesspool downriver. Entering it can seem life-threatening.

Positive decisions can bring us to the brink of the Poison River as well as negative ones. Choices such as marriage, moving, or starting a business can feel like Poison River crossings because they require change at the soul level. We may have glimpsed another realm in Stage Three and, in a sense, stand face-to-face with eternity. We arrive at the river bank, naked of what has sustained us in the past, and we must find a way to trust the unknown future even when logic says "no!" It is a time of testing, trial, and trust in an unknown future.

• THE TRICKSTER •

The Poison River marks our fall from innocence and self-absorption, from rote religion or mindless diversion into a specific task that we are being called to undertake. Something arrives to test our resolve, challenge our intention, demand our ingenuity. The Poison River is the precinct of the Trickster archetype, who may wear the sly face of evil one moment and look like a simpleton the next. The changing face of the river reflects the deeper currents at work.

In its most ancient form, the Trickster helped in the act of creation, stealing fire from the gods, botching the quest for immortality, or releasing bedeviling spirits into the world. According to

The Poison River

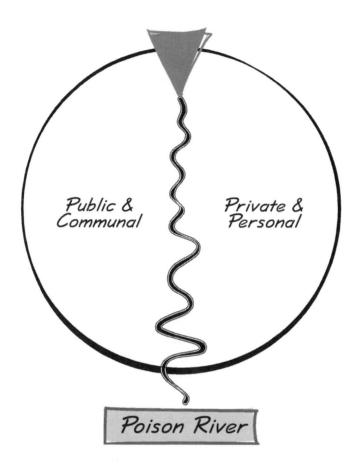

Leonard Biallas in *Myths: Gods, Heroes, and Saviors,* the Trickster or Clown helps us deal with forces we cannot control "without too much rationalization."[1] Where law and order prevail, the Trickster intrudes, upsets, disrupts, reminding us that soulwork is not about perfection. Just when we are ready to embark on the vision revealed in Stage Three, the Poison River reminds us of our vulnerability and dependence upon the spirit-world. That is the transforming work of the river.

Last winter my friend M. C. Richards painted a series of large, luminous iconic eggs. Beginning with a meditation on creativity for a class she was teaching, the sun came to her inner eye, and she recognized it as the creative center of our universe. Still in meditation, the sun became an egg yolk. "What could be a more persuasive image that our creativity is not a special gift, but a common, ordinary, built-in capacity?" she said. She began working with a luminous palette of metallic paints, and her large, simple egg forms glowed with energy—a core of yolk/sun/center in a field of copper, bronze, ruby, sapphire, and silver. Then one day the Trickster arrived. While working on a royal combination of deep purple and red, her brush took on a life of its own, splattering metallic gold like a broken yolk across the rich colors. "I was quite undone," she said, "and couldn't paint for several days."[2]

When she took up her brush again, the form of her painting had changed. Alive and spilling over smooth membrane lines, the icons flowed and heaved in tumult—even as her own energy surged and dropped. A trip to the doctor confirmed that two heart valves were worn out, not able to regulate the flow of blood through her heart. Over eighty but otherwise in good health, she knew surgery would be a risk, so she just kept painting, letting her soul questions guide her brush.

Unlike the expansive and eternal sense of Spirit in Stage Three, the Poison River brings us back to earth, to mortality, to sickness and the possibility of failure. Crossing the Poison River can be dangerous, particularly if the call we have heard seems impossible to accomplish or we sense the strength of opposing forces. Most mythical rivers do more than just drown. They are full of obstacles, mysterious foes, and unknown dangers, threatening death without rebirth. The image of water demands that, symbolically, we become the water-breathing creatures we once were in the womb. Water pulls us downward, into the primitive flow of life before air, before speech and song.

At this point in the soulwork cycle, we desperately need to know if God is really part of this call, because if the answer is "no," then we had better stay on the side of personal growth—tearing down our "father's altar" and building our own—but not testing the relationship with Spirit any further. To cross the Poison River, most of us need reassurance that we can trust that we *are* meant to go ahead, that we will *not* drown, that it is *God* who is calling us, and that God is *real* enough and powerful enough to accompany us on this journey. As my friend M.C. faced the question of whether to live with the uncertain flow of limited energy or to choose life-threatening surgery, one last painting in the series of iconic eggs flowed from her heart: a misty gray ground, alive with light where the form of an egg had been. Upward toward the edge, a nearly complete nimbus of bright light appeared around a darker moon. It looked like an image of spirit life to me, opening into a new call.

• *TESTING* •

In the biblical stories of Gideon and Esther, both needed to test their relationship with God as they entered the Poison River of permanent change. Gideon suffered another round of fear and indecision as the Hebrews began to gather in response to his decision for war against the Midianites. The possibility of success seemed to overwhelm him, and Gideon questioned God's presence. Even though he had ample evidence from earlier encounters with the angel and from his father's protection against death at the hands of a mob, Gideon still did not quite believe God would stay with him in battle. At this point, he could easily have slipped back into his old fearful self and begun the cycle again. Doubtful that he could proceed, Gideon proposed a foolproof test to reassure himself of God's power before trusting it completely.

It was one thing to have a private experience of angelic visitation and even to rebel against his father's belief system, but it was quite another to make battle plans with a motley group of tenant farmers against the army of Midian. Eliminating the angelic mediator, Gideon addressed God directly: "If you are really going to use me to save Israel as you promised, prove it to me in this way . . ." Gideon "threw a fleece" to test that God could deliver. Only when Gideon saw the tangible evidence of a wet sheepskin on dry ground, and then a dry sheepskin on wet ground, did he finally feel certain enough to plunge into his call.

Gideon's need for yet another test feels familiar to me. It suggests that our need for signs and reassurance is natural and normal. When I am about to make an important decision to leave behind my old security systems, I want some good evidence that the spiritual realm is reliable as a partner! I watch for a dream, look for coincidences, notice an unexpected call or connection with an old or new friend. This need for a test is not new. Again and again, the Bible describes weak and fallible human beings who needed reassurance that they could have a working relationship with the invisible powers beyond this world. Like us, ancient people questioned how they could be in relationship with God in practical situations.

Esther's test for God's presence took a different form. At this crossing point in her story, Esther turned inward. Mordecai had given her all the help and warning that he could. Nobody in the court knew she was Jewish, so she had no visible support there. The King's edict against the Jews would finally undermine what power she had as Queen, and she literally had no one left but God. When Esther decided to fast and pray for three days, she was entering a "dark night of the soul," clothed only with prayer and the stories of deliverance she had learned as a child. Entering the Poison River, she stripped off her royal robes, her symbols of royal power, to stand as a vulnerable human being in the presence of God. She faced the threat of death with full consciousness as she fasted and prayed, while her people did the same outside the castle walls.

Esther's prayer, which is found only in the Greek version, retold the story of Israel and its covenant relationship with God. Esther stood as a prophet, voicing her cry on behalf of her people. She railed against foreign gods who were "nonexistent beings." She prayed for courage. She claimed her power to face down "the lion" and did not sidestep the moral ambiguity of dealing with power and principalities. "You know I have never enjoyed this role," she reminded the Almighty. This prayer moved her from a personal dilemma into a heroic framework, inviting us to see the larger mythic dimension of her story.

• *STRIPPING DOWN* •

Crossing the Poison River can take years. It can also happen in a day or two. But it always involves "stripping down," leaving behind the stuff we have accumulated to reassure ourselves that we are lovable and capable. This is the point in a spiritual journey where we leave father and mother—or whatever substitute symbols (such as wealth, position, or relationships) we have clung to in the hope that they might provide meaning and purpose or rescue for us. Like pioneers moving West, we must unload the furniture we thought we needed when the journey began, leaving it behind on the trail for someone else to find.

When I was making the transition away from pottery toward religious retreat work, my husband's assignment to Germany felt like a Poison River crossing. My pottery co-op partners refused to hold my place if I went, and I was afraid that *not* going would cost me our marriage. What pushed me into the rushing waters was an offer to rent our house, furnished, if I could move out personal things. In one short week, I cleared the studio of greenware that I had thrown but not fired, stripped pictures from the walls and dishes from the cupboards, and shipped a minimal load of necessities to Germany. Suddenly I knew my work as a studio potter was done.

In order to cross the Poison River, we must trim down our baggage and cross with no excess. We review the story of what has brought us to this point, reassuring ourselves that the call has been real. We touch the objects that symbolize God's presence and look for a guide or a talisman for reassurance that God is with us. We carry the parts of our past that resonate with our call—songs, stories, traditions, dreams, images, icons. Our choice of what to take and what to leave behind will depend upon what we believe about the future.

• *CONFRONTING* •

The Poison River is the place where we confront our fears of failure and shame, of wasted life and needless death, where we listen for the voices of eternity and hear the voice of habitual roles tempting us to turn back and play our lives to ego development again and again.

Opposition or conflict may be the way the crossing comes. I think of my friend Vernon, who was charged with illegal handling of some outstanding debts that he had acquired when he bought a small manufacturing company. Because he is not a suspicious or cynical man, he had not been as careful in the transfer as he later learned to be. Thwarted at every turn, his trials were just beginning in the courtroom. Judged guilty, he was sentenced to sleep in the jail but keep the company running by day to pay the debts. In this Poison River, Vernon found resources in himself not previously needed. Although severely tested, he emerged not twisted by anger or regret. His time in jail proved to be the transit between his work and the cycle of discovering his gifts for the world.

Crossing the Poison River often feels like dying because we leave our familiar supports behind. To enter the waters, we, like Esther, have to confront our fears of death and endings, whether great or small. Our existential fear is that nobody will notice or care. If our dying, whether figurative or factual, has a larger purpose, we are more likely to enter the unknown and see it as birth instead of death. We cannot know the outcome, the final form, but we can know we are part of something much larger and more complex than what we can imagine or control. We can enter the Poison River only by faith, trusting our intuition and feelings as part of the process.

In Hermann Hesse's book *Siddhartha* the hero lives through multiple trials and temptations on his way to understanding what life is all about. Finally he is schooled by an old boatman, who learned peace from the river itself. Siddhartha grows in his feel for the river moving away from doctrines and teachings, clever words, and the notion that wisdom can be taught. He simplifies his life more and more, grieving that he cannot save his son from going through the same trials that he himself traversed. In the end, he teaches with silence by receiving a kiss. This moment of touch provides the bridge between two old friends on rival paths.[3] Crossing the river is the major metaphor of this little classic, published in 1951. I read it in high school and frequently returned to its puzzling message as I struggled through my first two journeys around the soulwork cycle, facing the questions, *"Who am I?"* and *"What is my work?"*

Real or imagined, stories such as *Siddhartha* help us enter the Poison River vicariously, releasing emotions, exciting our imagination, letting us "try on" a new identity. A book or a movie—such as the Titanic disaster story that resurfaces in popular imagination every few years—can often be a vehicle to help us engage the real feelings and questions that are emerging for us. We are fascinated by the way natural disasters reveal the range of human behavior, how each character deals with the possibility of rescue or death. We long to know what the other side will be like. Archetypal stories of death and resurrection can feed the spirit. Sacramental celebrations like the Eucharist or communion can be the vehicle for crossing. Images from nature can reassure us of new birth. Music can provide clues to the state of our soul. Confronting our fears can be as simple and difficult as picking up a paintbrush to begin a new canvas.

• *TRUSTING* •

The critical element in crossing the Poison River is trust. What we believe about what is on the other side is crucial. In a real sense, the question of call is always one of belief, and the Poison River point in the cycle challenges our basic patterns. Are we alive just to get through another day? Or is there a larger meaning to life? Is there a call to bring justice and mercy into being for ourselves and others? Or is it every one for himself or herself? Are there evil forces that must be confronted? Or is anything all right as long as it does not kill someone else? What does make human life a valuable part of creation? Why make any sacrifice beyond getting more for ourselves?

What we believe about God in this passage will influence our ability to claim the call to newness. If we hold a mechanical view based on control and predictability, we will discount the cycle of call and keep our spiritual life separate from our work in the world. But if the cosmic story of ongoing creation rings through us, as it did for Esther and Gideon, we will be able to live into an unknown future with curiosity, transcending old systems that box and label experience in a predetermined way.

At one of my workshops, a woman spoke with great distress about wanting to leave her job, but she was afraid to let go of the income. She was in sales, and what she was selling did not fit with her values or her vision for humanity. "What should I do?" she asked. The temptation was great for me to take on the mantle of expert and tell her what to do. I would be lying to say that it is not flattering to be asked such a question, but generally my answer is something like this: "I don't know what you should do. Pray for a sign." When she persisted, I suggested some practices that might encourage trust: "Watch your dreams for an image. Practice meditation. Let your imagination wander. Pare down your dependence on what your income is supporting. Develop your ability to trust God for this passage and don't push out in the boat before you are ready to embrace the risk ahead. There is nothing to prove." That may be the hardest part to comprehend: *There is nothing to prove*, no time-keeper with a stopwatch to judge whether we got an early or late start, no "winner's" circle. Following call is its own reward.

The way of fear leads to accumulation, grasping for security, efforts at control, isolation, and brutality. Deciding to follow God's call leads to freedom and peace. But when we are entering the Poison River, the way looks perilous indeed.

• *TEMPTATIONS* •

An archetypal Poison River story is the New Testament account of Jesus and his temptations after forty days of fasting.[4] Just before Jesus was about to make his ministry public, he was baptized in the River Jordan by his cousin, John. It was a crossing point between his private spiritual preparation and the beginning of much public scrutiny. Immediately after his baptism, Jesus was led into the desert by the Spirit where he was tempted by Satan. In this case, both Spirit and Satan appear to be Trickster figures.

The biblical picture of wilderness is not the quiet place where one goes for retreat, but a desolate place with no food or water, a time of testing and endurance, letting go of fantasy and finding a way through trials. In the language of the soulwork cycle, the devil tempted Jesus to stay "spiritual," to remain in Stage Three, instead of crossing the threshold into living out the purpose of his life.

In the first temptation, Satan urged Jesus to turn stones into bread, to use his spiritual power to satisfy his own hunger rather than that of the outcasts from the religious system of his culture. In the second temptation, Satan promised Jesus power over all the kingdoms of the world "if you will worship me." This temptation to worship "other gods" instead of the Creator is a temptation we are faced with daily in the form of material possessions, societal successes, or technological thrills. The third temptation for Jesus was to deny his mortality, to by-pass death. That, too, is a temptation that modern technology seems to put before us, diverting us from the question of what to use our life energy *for*, to how we can use our energy to *avoid* death or discomfort. To deny our humanity and avoid the limits imposed by our bodies are the basic temptations at the middle of every soulwork cycle.

The temptations to sidestep call come to us in many ways, but ultimately they boil down to the three forms in Jesus' story: focusing on only our own needs; worshipping at the throne of worldly success; and wanting to avoid death and endings by side-stepping our human limits.

• ENCOURAGEMENT •

It is popular now to think that we create our own reality and can live without limits, but the biblical story of Jesus clearly points to another truth: We must live within the limits of our mortality, recognize our vulnerability . . . and make the crossing anyway. The good news of God's call is that we do not have to do it alone. Always there is a helper, a guide, or a fellow pilgrim to share the crossing. Spirit comes—if not in person, then in a dream or vision or sense of right timing. The Poison River is a place of infinite disguise, of shifting shapes and shadowy fears. This may also be the place where we can meet Christ as Spirit in a form we never expected —as a beggar, a clown, or a child.

When a community or group or church becomes a place to share those wilderness experiences, we help each other make the crossing. At our Seekers Church, a government lawyer shared his temptation to stay where he was, in a position of privilege and power, rather than plunging into the Poison River of call to do something about making the political system more open to others:

I confess that I am bound in "golden handcuffs" of salary, and position, and standard of living, and American culture and race and maleness. When Seekers first engaged in dialogue about racism and feminism, I knew that, as a white, male, American lawyer, I had unfair advantages. I envisioned a fulcrum of social policy and Christianity at the end where I stood, that could pivot up those who were disadvantaged—women, people of color, non-Americans.

But then I became aware that the radical challenge of the gospel is to think of the fulcrum in the middle—to bring me down from that privileged place as it lifts others up.

And a few weeks ago in our social justice class, Peter Bankson pointed out that the fulcrum might be over at the other end, so that the mountain on which I stand is leveled. And I have to ask myself, 'Do I want to prepare the way for the kind of Messiah who calls me to be a servant like him, one who chose not to cling to equality with God, but to humble himself even unto death?' [5]

In these words, the lawyer moved from resist—hoping others would be raised to his level of comfort . . . to reclaim—seeing that he might have to let go of privilege in order to raise others . . . to revelation—that the whole system might have to dissolve. In the space of a few short sentences, he stood at the Poison River, questioning his ability to move forward by faith.

Being in a community with other people who are willing to leave familiar ground for the unknown is an encouragement. It can also be terrifying if we are not ready to embark on that journey ourselves. Knowing that we—or others around us—have been this way before is one benefit of understanding and sharing the soulwork cycle.

• *FROM PRIVATE TO PUBLIC* •

To cross the Poison River from private spirituality into public action, seekers in every tradition have used engagement and detachment. The Western tradition of engagement and embodiment of Spirit presents the Poison River as a real barrier but not a permanent one—waters that we can pass through with God's help, much as the Hebrews passed through the Red Sea in their escape from Pharaoh's Egypt. Gideon engaged the situation by "throwing a fleece" and challenging God to provide observable proof of power over the physical world. However, the Eastern tradition of detachment is also part of the discipline we need to cross the river. Esther withdrew in prayer, detaching from her earthly symbols of power and prestige. To be in relationship with God does not mean we have to choose one way or the other.

In the past few years, there has been a stream of books from both Eastern and Western religious traditions guiding us toward a healthy balance of inward discipline and outward witness. Henri Nouwen's life and books have tutored a generation of seekers who have sought the inner disciplines woven through the first three stages of the soulwork cycle in order to sustain some kind of public ministry, as Nouwen did in his work with handicapped adults. Thich Nhat Hahn's book *Living Buddha, Living Christ* bears witness to the power of Buddhist detachment from the terrifying threats of war and a social worker's involvement with the most vulnerable population caught in civil upheaval—the children. A gift from the monastic traditions of both Christianity and Buddhism has been their attention to spiritual practice: daily habits of intentional focus on Spirit. Those are the "daily disciplines" that mold us from the inside out and give us the courage to enter the transforming river, whatever the results will be. Perhaps one of the tasks of the new millennium is crossing the Poison River that has separated these Eastern and Western religious traditions.

While detachment is part of the task, paying attention to God's leading and promise of relationship is the core of call to the future. God needs our physicality to taste and touch, to see and hear and love, to be conscious of good and evil. Our humanity has a purpose, and crossing the Poison River is a choice to bring that Divine Spirit into the world of hungers unmet, of power unchecked, and of life imperfectly lived. In the Judeo-Christian tradition, the physicality of Jesus and his teachings about the realm of God "on earth as in heaven" suggest that we can bring the *kairos* realm into being by engaging with the pain and evil of this world because we trust in the creative power of God flowing through us.

• *CROSSING OVER* •

Reaching the far shore of the Poison River can seem like the end of a cycle instead of the midpoint. As we have traversed the first three stages, we have suffered through trials, withstood tests, and learned to trust, even as we have developed a deeper sensitivity about what not to trust. In crossing the Poison River, the Trickster may have plagued the journey with false hopes or shifting sandbars that were nothing more than temporary resting spots. Yet here we stand . . . on the far shore, ready for the journey ahead.

If we are in our first round of the soulwork cycle—as Busters defining who we are—the river crossing will bring us to a commitment to person or to a path that separates us from those we love, testing severely our sense of identity.

If we are in our second round of the soulwork cycle—as Boomers finding our work in the world—the Poison River will bring us to take on a challenge that college or family did not prepare us for.

If we are in our third round—as Bridgers seeking what our gift for the world might be—the River will bring us to a test, like Vernon's jail sentence, that calls for a more serious application of our gifts than we have been using in our work.

And if we are in our fourth round of the soulwork cycle—as Builders creating the legacy we want to leave behind us—the Poison River often boils up as a physical symptom that requires deeper soulwork than we have been challenged with before.

Each time we cross the Poison River, we face the temptation to separate body and spirit, to turn back and replay old roles rather than push ahead with the tangible physical integration that soul seeks. Each time, we deepen the connection between *kairos* and *chronos* time, able to live our daily lives with a consciousness we have not had before.

• • •

At this crucial "crossing point" in the cycle of call, I have found the following simple practice helpful. Consider taking some time to:

> *Sit quietly and focus on your breathing.*
> *Become aware of the barrier*
> *between your spirit life*
> *and what you do each day.*
> *Let your heart open*
> *to learn what your next step is.*

• • •

Stage Four: RISK

CHAPTER 7

Silence is like a rudder through choppy seas. When I remember to stop and breathe, I can reconnect with God. Words drop away like old clothes. I am naked and new again, supple as clay in the Potter's hands. Maybe a dozen times a day I stop and breathe, look and listen, refocus my attention beyond habitual response. Often an image arrives or words pop into my head, like manna for the moment. Refreshed, I can risk a new way.

Deep within us is planted the seed of new creation—dreams for a better world and wild hope that our visions can be realized. We have an unquenchable need for new life, new forms, new ideas to be realized in Stage Four. In the first three stages of the soulwork cycle, we can keep our private sense of call secret and separate from others who might object or oppose what we are feeling drawn to do. But in Stage Four, call shifts from a private conversation with God to a public form of some kind. If we have smashed old altars in the third stage, we will have to take new risks in the fourth. We will have to trust previously undeveloped parts of our selves to bring the vision of Stage Three into being. It may mean taking only a small step at first, but we need to *act* to make our dreams come true.

External commitment to an internal call feels risky because it requires that we move from an old framework of values into a new one that may not be very coherent at this point. New actions do not automatically bring other people into alignment with our dreams or drives. We can expect opposition from old friends or people invested in the status quo.

At a systemic level, any change in the status quo will evoke opposition, especially if money is involved. The risk of moving forward with call includes learning to articulate our vision for change, dealing with opposition that may be unconscious and therefore unnamed, and developing strategies for protecting the seeds of newness that may be tender and somewhat fragile.

At a personal level, our fears may flash out as anger or sink new ventures in a morass of depression. I remember calling my mother just as my first book was being published. I was awash with anxiety about whether she would be able to accept the things I had written about my early life. At the moment of publication, I felt as if I were a little girl again, wanting my mother's approval. Aware that my sisters had produced grandchildren for her and I had not, I told her, "This feels a bit like giving birth. A real baby is winsome and can be easily forgiven for not being perfect, but somehow a printed page seems harder to love. I hope you'll love it anyway." I realized that part of my early resistance to following my call to write had been fear of exposure. At this stage I was ready to be more visible . . . though not without trying to bring my parent's approval into the new world I was creating with my words.

Each time we come round the soulwork cycle on the spiral journey, the risk we face in Stage Four will be different, but the life-and-death feeling of it will always be the same. It is in this stage

Stage 4: Risk

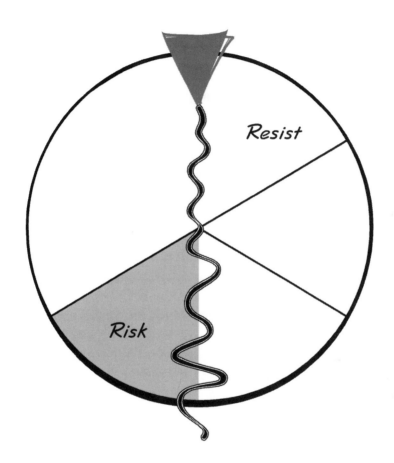

that our call can overcome our fear, take possession of our resources and hopes, and move us into action. This is the stage of "firsts": beginning a new job, going back to school, offering a concert in public, taking a stand on some issue, moving after the death of a spouse or parent.

To begin a new venture based on call means sharing it aloud, inviting others to care about something we have carried inside. Countless luncheons or phone conversations may yield a partner, someone to shoulder the vision with us. A small group of investors may put money down on an idea or we may finally talk with an editor after many rejection slips. Even the decision to redecorate a room can be a sign of reaching this step of moving from theory to practice, turning revelation into reality, shifting possibility into practicality.

The work at Stage Four of the soulwork cycle requires that we stay in touch with the spiritual guidance that prompted our call from the beginning. As we get involved in the details of performance, it is easy to lose sight of Spirit. This is where some accountability structure can be helpful: a spiritual director, a therapist, a faithful friend with whom we have made a specific commitment.

In the tradition of The Church of the Saviour, Seekers Church suggests that people in Stage Four seek a partner to share in the birthing of a new call. If we do it alone, there is great danger that our ego involvement will mean more focus on "success" than on "faithfulness," that we will short circuit the "bigness" of call because we cannot sustain it alone. Midwifing a new project requires stamina, dedication, and a partner for encouragement as well as complementary skills.

My friend Anne told me about one of her dreams, as she struggled to write a book:

> *I am walking in the woods and come to a swampy area. I am standing at the edge, wondering how to get across. If I walk through, my boots will be wet and dirty for the remainder of my hike. If I take off my boots, I will get my feet dirty and have to feel the ooze, which frightens and disgusts me. Just then, you come walking up, we exchange a few words and then you simply walk through the muck. I watch, feel encouraged and do that too.*[1]

Because the risk of call is more often "swampy" than clear, in Stage Four we need soul guides to wade ahead of us in the murky water, to sink into the ooze, to get "down and dirty" with us for the sake of moving ahead. Though we may still be afraid and hesitant, soul guides can help us face what we dread, fear, or reject as we move into the creative muck of form and feeling.

• RESISTANCE REDIRECTED •

Risk in Stage Four is the counterpart of resistance in Stage One. Risk turns the energy of resistance into action. Instead of pushing the call away, we turn, like a Tai Chi student, to join the direction of energy flowing from the call. Our crossing of the Poison River has marked our decision to let the old ways go and begin a new venture. The vision and responsibility that we feared in the beginning has become an ally. We have traded the stagnation of resistance for the results of risk. We are now ready to move toward something larger than ego expression.

In Stage Four, we turn from longing for escape into the ether of abstraction and imagination, toward the sensuous reality of taste, touch, and tone. This is the embodied realm where decisions come with cost and commitment. Taking the risk of producing something new returns us to the present moment, for *now* is the only time we have for action. If the Innocent's question of God in Stage One is "Who are you?" then God's question of us in Stage Four is, "And who are *you?*" It is time to take a stand.

We live in a culture that likes newness, welcomes innovation, and depends upon our soul's restlessness to fuel acquisition. Taking risks is culturally sanctioned, particularly when economic gain might be the result. People buy lottery tickets, gamble on the stock market, buy things on "time," and regularly break speed limits as though time could be saved. But Stage Four is more than innovation. Response to call is a deeper decision to trust inner guidance and make it visible to others. With clarity and urgency that comes from our connection to what is life-giving, the risks we take in this stage are known best by the heart.

• *BIRTHING* •

In an essay titled "What Is Our Work?," Margaret Wheatley writes, "At the very heart of our ideas about life is this definition, that life begins from the desire to create something original, to bring a new being into form."[2] Risk is built into being alive. While it is popular in religious and psychological settings to denigrate our "doing" and emphasize the transcendence of "being" in the presence of God, Stage Four requires action. We must move from the realm of abstraction and dreams into the physical realm of risk and results.

Risk is ultimately a birthing stage, often marked by sweat, blood, and tears, along with moments of ecstatic joy. Something tangible becomes visible and begins to breathe. Our creativity finds form and substance. We sound a call for some new initiative and hope others will respond. Some go from gestation to birth with painful contractions, making this a difficult and anxious stage. Some enter this stage triumphant, just glad to be rid of doubt and indecision. For them, risk feels like a long-awaited adventure. Others feel timid and hesitant, afraid to act and yet more afraid to go back. Most feel relieved but spent with the effort of crossing the Poison River. We may feel ready to start small, take a first step, risk failure, shame, and embarrassment on behalf of a larger vision, but at the same time, we hope it will not end that way.

In Gordon Cosby's words, we are seized by the power of a great affection.[3] We are drawn to possibility like a magnet, willing to risk everything for the possibility of bringing something new into being. During the civil rights era of the late sixties, Gordon focused on children in Washington, D.C. A movement began to close Junior Village, a "dumping ground" for truant, disabled, and otherwise unwanted children. Out of that campaign grew FLOC (For Love of Children), a Church of the Saviour mission incorporated separately as a nonprofit. As other missions formed out of Gordon's passion for the poor, he began to push for each mission to become a separate congregation to preserve the intensity of Stage Four, rather than becoming more bureaucratic and building a bigger church. In 1976, the director of FLOC paired with a volunteer from their foster-care support group, Hope and a Home, to issue a call for The Seekers Church. Five other little churches formed at the same time, each with a separate mission focus. Few churches risk such multiple births to focus on call.

Sometimes the risk of beginning a new venture is an act of desperation where all other choices have been taken away. I recently got a letter in which a woman described her journey from a glamorous life on the "fast track," to the crisis of a life-threatening illness and a cry for help, to a new beginning based on the Twelve-Step program of Alcoholics Anonymous. She had just begun to realize that this was a path of spiritual birthing. Her story is a reminder that the risk arising out of call is not a temporary high, but a decision to reorient our life, to bring something new into the world, and take responsibility for it.

Birth is a time of contraction and peril, of pushing and pain, of blood and uncertainty. After months, maybe years, of darkness and waiting and struggle, we are ready to give birth to newness. Every artist knows that process. Each birth has its own dynamic energy, its own timing and sequence. Each of us carries a cellular memory of the journey from possibility into life and breath and being. We are indeed born again and again as we dare to believe that change can happen because we decide to act.

• *RITUAL* •

This beginning of the second half of the soulwork cycle calls for some kind of ritual to mark the birth of something new in our lives. When we give birth to call in the public realm, ritual moves our risk beyond personal anguish into community consciousness, and we can tap the power of our shared humanity. Rituals represent our connection to the unseen realm of Spirit. Our rituals may be simple: lighting a candle, meeting a friend for golf, sewing a garment, signing a contract, starting a new journal, or calling a press conference. Rituals may also have to mark the loss of something in order to celebrate a new beginning. As one woman described the risk she was taking at a personal level, she revealed the origin of her call to the child welfare system as well:

> *I was in the dance class . . . The exercise that we did one night was an authentic movement witnessed by a partner . . . and the movement [she] witnessed was of me cradling a baby and then putting it down and leaving it behind. Within a week of that movement, I miscarried.*
>
> *Few people knew the grief that I felt. Few people knew the depth of the wilderness then, the lack of life, the dryness, and the longing for comfort. Because I had not been open about the pregnancy, how could I share about the miscarriage? Because people hadn't seen a physical change in me, how could I share my grief?*
>
> *At times, the wilderness for me was my own aloneness with my feelings about what had happened. But I couldn't keep the pain inside. I turned to members of this community to share the burden of grief: my mission group first, some people in the School of Christian Living, a gathering of women who made the baby quilt for Casey. I also turned to the work of my hands as a way to work out my grief. I needed to make a quilt that represented where I was, what I was feeling, what I hoped. It was a way I could work through pain. I began the quilt just a week after my miscarriage.[4]*

As this woman stood before us, unfolding the intricate pattern of cream, grays, and browns of her quilt, we saw how she had given birth in another way. She had allowed the impulse of creativity to rise and take form in color and cloth. As her words and quilt told her story, she claimed the power of public ritual, giving her loss a larger context. The child-not-born took form in this lovely quilt and in her work for children as a civil servant.

In a culture that values verbal and rational skills, handwork often expresses the language of soul. In school, we learn to sit still and exercise our brains, separating body and spirit, inner and outer life. We lose touch with pleasure and passion, substituting power or success for the call to birth something new from our bodyselves. Taking time for art, for music, for poetry can be a way to cultivate our growth at this stage in the soulwork cycle. Making something new represents a clear departure from the past. We may not know exactly what we are making because it will have a life of its own. Who can describe how creation comes into being? In Stage Four, we take the risk of bringing Spirit into a living, breathing form of being. Soulwork drops down to the belly, where breathing centers the body in a deeper kind of knowing and creativity can be sustained—even though the final form is not yet assured.

• *A WARRIOR'S FOCUS* •

Because we live with finite limits in time and space, whenever we give birth to something new, other things have to be set aside. Saying "yes" to something new requires that we say "no" to other possibilities, which are not necessarily bad or evil, just roads not taken. In a culture where we want to "keep our options open," call requires focus. We must say "good-bye" to myriad possibilities in order to say "hello" to something specific—a child, a new mate, a job or health decision, a political act to change the status quo. This kind of commitment requires a Warrior's focus.

In myth, the Warrior archetype contains both creative and destructive energy. Leonard Biallas says that the destructive elements of a Warrior's quest—destroying cities, conquering demons, and slaying monsters—are all secondary to the inward transformation that is taking place.[5] In popular culture, the Warrior's paradoxical power of creation and destruction is played out in the *Star Wars* movie classic, when young Luke Skywalker battles with

Darth Vader, whom we later learn is Luke's father. Luke's creative energy struggles with Darth Vader's destructive power. Luke's physical and spiritual preparation pays off, but just barely. At the crux of the story, as they face each other in hand-to-hand combat, Luke commits all of his faculties, all of his resources, to this battle and no other. It is this singular focus that marks his shift from training to performance, from possibility to practice.

The need for a Warrior's focus and commitment took an unusual turn in the biblical story of Gideon. When he decided to battle the Midianites as God had commanded, a sizable army gathered. Then Gideon heard an absurd direction that required all of his commitment and trust: "Reduce the number of soldiers so you will know victory is not your own doing."

Paring a project down to its essential elements is one of the disciplines of call, but it may not feel natural or prudent. Surely Gideon must have wondered about the angel's directive to dismiss thousands of potential warriors. For us, paring down to essentials may seem no less absurd. Because we live in a culture that assumes "more is better," the discipline of pruning away unnecessary parts before proceeding may seem ridiculous, terrifying, or impossible. Just when we have decided to commit all of our resources to the task at hand, God says "focus on one thing and depend on me." It seems foolhardy in the face of tremendous odds.

Discernment about what to discard and what to save is a spiritual question in tension with cultural messages about how much security we need or want. Especially if we have stripped down to cross the Poison River, having plenty of reserves would seem logical in Stage Four. Gideon wanted to use all the volunteers who came, but the angel knew better and, in an act of supreme trust, Gideon obeyed the angel's prompt. Call preempts caution in this stage.

Gideon sent home anyone who was "fearful and trembling." Twenty-two thousand went and ten thousand remained, but God said that was still too many. Gideon was then instructed to take his volunteers to a stream and send home those who looked down as they lapped water "like dogs." He was to keep only those who cupped the water in their hands. We can only guess that they were the ones who might be the more vigilant, the more alert to the dangers they were facing. Just when Gideon wanted a huge army in order to look powerful enough to scare his enemies, God deflated his ego! God did not want Gideon to think he had accomplished the upcoming victory by his own genius. With only three hundred volunteers left, the risk for Gideon was the public humiliation of a defeat in battle.

After two rounds of trimming his army to a small number, Gideon was probably in desperate need of reassurance. "If you are still afraid to attack," God told him, "go into the camp of your enemies and you will be encouraged." There Gideon heard the Midianites bemoaning a dream in which their commander's tent had been demolished by a rolling loaf of barley bread, signifying their destruction by their food source, the Israelites.

With this preposterous image, we get a glimpse of God's perspective. The dream prepared the way for Gideon's attack. His worry was normal—but not essential. His focus needed to shift from his own strength to the larger creative purpose taking place through his efforts.

In whatever small or large way we are called to risk a new venture, we, too, need to draw on the Warrior's sense of focus. Qualities of watchfulness, readiness, and awareness must come to the foreground while that which is "fearful and trembling" is released or set aside. Our resources may not be reduced to a minimum as Gideon's were, but we still must listen for the guidance that comes once we have decided to trust our call.

A spiritual practice that combines physical centering and prayerful openness can help us weed out wasteful and unproductive issues that might distract us from our commitment. Whenever we buck tradition, such focus is essential. Any risk of action that goes against or beyond popular tastes requires that we be exquisitely present and attentive to the reality of what is.

• *A WARRIOR'S COURAGE* •

In the stories of Esther and Gideon, the Warrior archetype is expressed in different ways. In Esther's story, we witness another quality of the Warrior as she put on her queenly garments and went into the King's chamber uninvited. In comparison to the effort she had made to prepare herself for this moment, the event was almost anticlimactic. *The Jerusalem Bible* tells us, "[The King's] face blazed with anger . . . and she began to faint." Her courage failed. Her body wilted, and she seemed on the verge of collapse. But in that moment the King's heart was changed, and he rushed to Esther's side, ready to hear what had caused her to take such a risk.

At first glance, Esther's action is an old story of female manipulation: she fainted and he rescued. But Esther, listening intently for God's sense of right timing, pursued her goal. She asked the King and his chief-of-staff, her nemesis, Haman, to come to her chambers for a private dinner. On the surface, she had risked death for a dinner party! At a deeper level, however, Esther was taking one step at a time to accomplish the larger call that Mordecai had given her—to save her people.

We see here a woman brought to the very edge of her human capacity, bearing the burden of her call into the face of extreme danger. Such heroism is not often demanded of us, we think, and yet, over and over again I hear stories from men and women who, like Esther, are willing to face their fears and take their lives in their own hands—to enter therapy, start a new business, bear a child into the world, confront public officials, and otherwise act with courage when the easy way would be to set aside their dreams of living out their call. Giving birth in whatever form it happens is an act of courage!

The Warrior archetype is not about conformity, but about the courage to change. I can think of no greater courage than the courage required to take responsibility for our power to hurt others, as well as our power to create healing. Every parent has that power. In fact, we all have the Warrior's power to hurt as well as heal. In the

Twelve-Step Program of AA, this stage of call is realized when we "humbly ask for change" and "are willing to make amends." Humility suggests *humus*, earthiness, sharing our humanity, not our godlike notions of superiority or separateness. Being "willing to make amends" marks the shift from inner awareness to outward action that is not dependent upon approval or acceptance by others. If we are conscious of God's call to be part of a cosmic drama in which good and evil vie for primacy in human affairs, even the most humble act of creation or reconciliation will have eternal overtones. It takes courage to stand for what we believe.

• *A WARRIOR'S INTUITION* •

For the archetypal Warrior, intuition is the guiding power. No plan or strategy is sufficient for the mythic terrain of the soul. No preparation is complete enough to cover all the challenges that call for a deeper kind of guidance, an inner sort of knowing. Jean Shinoda Bolen, in *Goddesses in Every Woman*, portrays Athena as a Warrior with powers of destruction and creation. Bolen pictures Athena with a spear in one hand and a spindle in the other. Athena serves as the patron military forces as well as patron of weavers, potters, and goldsmiths. Her powers are intuitive, and tangible results are her particular gifts.[6]

Linking the power of Athena's intuition and focus, a friend from Seekers used Athena's Warrior qualities to describe her sense of call and risk in becoming a weaver:

When I choose colors and patterns, I have the sensation that I am making decisions in a new and unfamiliar way. My energy is moving downward in my body. My weaving decisions seem to come from the place below my rib cage, my solar plexus. I try many possibilities before one feels right and I stay with it. Once the decision has been made, I proceed with a steadiness that is also unfamiliar to me. I do not need to work with rules. Slowly, through trial and error, I have come to realize that I have an inner guide that understands harmony and knows when the feeling is right. Weaving is the first time in my life that I have been able to gain faith in this guide. As I experiment with colors and patterns, I like myself better. I discover that I have an imagination after all. I am willing to try the unexpected and occasionally it works.[7]

Using a Warrior's intuition is not restricted to launching a new career or taking a risky public action. Sometimes we exercise the trust involved in Stage Four in smaller ways. Every time I go on a trip, for example, I lay out what I think I might want with as much intuition and forethought as I can muster. I choose a manageable bag for the trip I am anticipating and pare down my stuff to what I can carry. Frequently I prune too much and am forced into creative solutions—and I like it that way. It depends on whether the trip is about comfort and control of the unknown or whether it is a chance to experience new questions and challenges in a creative way. I want to choose the latter as an ongoing school for my soul.

• BEYOND RISK •

Risk requires that we be willing to fail as well as succeed, to be wrong as well as right. Risking failure is the doorway to consciousness, the anthem of our humanity. And while it may look to the observer that we have learned to trust ourselves when we put our call in the public eye, we have, in fact, begun to trust something deeper, more mysterious and powerful, which in turn frees us to act in ways that may seem foolish, even foolhardy, to others.

Listening to inner guidance may take us away from the dominant culture, away from the easy acquiescence to "the way things are" into the realm of possibility, demanding commitment to whatever comes. Having a partner can help us detach from the ego investment that risk automatically entails. We may find that we can share our discoveries with a few who want to move forward with us, while we leave behind those people who cannot make the jump to a new reality.

Going public in Stage Four with what has previously been only private and personal brings us to leaving excess safety and moving into an unknown situation. Both creator and destroyer energies of the Warrior are brought together in a powerful struggle for the birth of something new. Knowing that the spiral journey of call regularly brings us to this point can be comforting and empowering. If we are on our second or third round of the soulwork cycle, we can step back and recognize that we have been here before and can trust ourselves to the process.

Stage Five: RELATE

CHAPTER 8

Will anyone care when I'm gone? Does my life make a differ-
ence to others? Without children, I don't have any "auto-
matic" connections. All must be cultivated and cared for. I
know I need both people and place for belonging, to say what I
believe and be held accountable for it. I can look back and see
that "doing my own thing" is satisfying only for a short while.
It's the relational side of call that gets shortchanged in our in-
dividualistic culture.

The birthing of call, like all births, needs a family, a
community context in which to thrive and grow. That is the
essence of Stage Five—discovering and building those
surrounding relationships. We know what impact a new baby has
on a whole network of relationships: parents, friends, grand-
parents, local community. Everyone makes adjustments around a
birth. Soulwork has that effect, too. When we change from the

inside out, everyone around us is affected in some way. It is in Stage Five that our framework for decision-making expands to include others. They may be people who are not directly involved in the risks we have decided to take. They may be a different set of people than those we depended on in earlier stages. But we need the "otherness" of people who share facets of a single whole if we are to recover the sacredness of life.

Like the tendency of single-cells to multiply and organize, there is a natural transition from singular risks to some organizational form. What began as a unique and personal invitation to newness will spread to others. Our task in Stage Five is to connect with a larger community who can share in our sense of purpose, find a common language, common symbols, and a common story. Call carries us beyond personal achievement into an organizational form. This stage requires community for celebration, correction, and systemic impact.

People researching the connection between spirit and health are discovering the vital importance of relationship and community. We are created for connection and not isolation. Relationships are critically important in the work of Elizabeth Kubler Ross with terminally ill patients, and Bernie Siegel with cancer survivors. Searching for heart disease remedies, Dean Ornish, who once focused on diet and exercise to control cholesterol, now cites relationships as the critical factor for good health.

While many people assume that life-giving relationships must develop outside of the workplace, perceptive observers know we cannot live out our deepest values in one place and not another. "We're herd animals," Richard Heckler says emphatically in his book *Holding the Center*. Heckler describes the basic elements of a functional community as (a) willingness to see and be seen, (b) work toward a common goal, (c) a shared practice the supports a perspective on the world, and (d) commitment to work through hard times.[1] To see and be seen suggests the necessity for witness and mirroring. Work toward a common goal requires that the purpose of the group be clear and openly stated. Having a shared practice that reflects our worldview (such as worship or regular spiritual disciplines) reveals whether the group is functioning with a mechanical or a relational perspective. And, finally, the commitment to engage one another during the difficult times reveals the resiliency of community connections.

It is in Stage Five that we are drawn back to the basic commonality of belonging to a larger living network of relationships. For the soul, relating is not just healthier, it is critical.

• *COUNTERPART OF RECLAIM* •

In many ways, relating to a new community based on a different understanding of God in Stage Five puts flesh and blood on the stories and traditions reclaimed in Stage Two. Both stages are collective and communal. What quickens as remembrance in Stage Two becomes the link for relating in Stage Five.

When Mordecai asked Esther for her help, she was challenged to reclaim her connection with her Jewish heritage. In Stage Five, Esther put her call into collective action, getting the King to allow her people a chance to defend themselves. In Gideon's story, the successful battle that took place in Stage Five was prefigured by his reclaiming the close connection his people once had with Yahweh.

For us, reclaiming parts of our own story that we may have rejected begins to take on some new organizational form in the world in Stage Five. We may start or join a group that will encourage the call we have claimed. We may join a church, form a task force, organize a local chapter of a wider movement. Relating to others around call will probably be a place where we can "tell our story" in different ways. It will always be a place where we can take action in concert with others on behalf of some larger vision of what life is for.

Stage 5: Relate

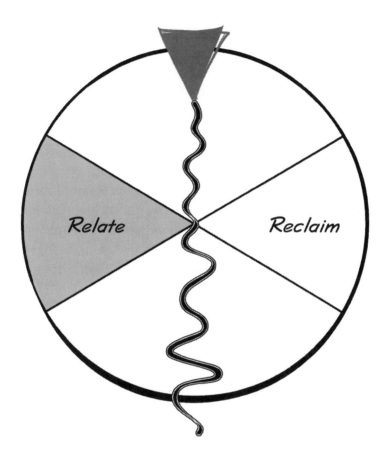

• *ORGANIC vs. MECHANICAL WORLDVIEW* •

Long before modern cosmologists began writing about a relational worldview based on quantum physics, the biblical story portrayed God as one who calls ordinary people into leadership and action within community. The biblical image of community is like a body energized by the soul of call. Each part has a different function, different needs, and different connection with the whole. Ideally, people who share their call become a such community, sharing gifts, honing sensitivities for mutual creativity, and being shaped by one another and the Spirit in the process. Yet it would be inaccurate to imagine that community means uniformity. A called community will always includes people we do not like, who reflect our shadow side. One of the gifts of soulwork is learning to live and work with people unlike ourselves. To the extent that our understanding of call is informed by this radical image of being part of a single body, the structures we create do impact the possibility of living out of call. Organic communities will always be in flux because every time something new is added, the whole relational structure must adjust.

In reality, our culture works against organic community. We have been taught that economic organizations cannot function this way because it limits predictability and quality control. Businesses try to operate within a mechanical model where people are treated as interchangeable parts. In this worldview, people are motivated by competition, privacy, entitlement, rights, individualism, and a ladder of success that has room for only one on top. The mechanical model gathers individuals into large, faceless conglomerates, spitting out standardized menus / stores / cars / television programs to keep the economic engines going. Those on the inside denigrate care for outsiders, clinging to the fantasy that everyone can enjoy a high standard of living if they just work hard enough.

Even in our schools, while we give lip service to education as a place to encourage creativity, standardized tests give way to standardized work in which we deny the necessity for adjustment to one another. In fact, our school system teaches us more about control and power than relationship. We learn to behave "properly," sit in straight rows, psyche out the teacher, memorize what is required, cut corners, do as little as we can. Even when a school develops service projects to encourage relationship between school and neighborhood, we rarely see the resources of caring and imagination turned in the direction of seeing the community as a living system. Churches are not often different, even though the biblical model of community is organic and familial rather than mechanical. Emphasis on church growth and structures of control more often repeat cultural patterns in the church than cultivate an atmosphere in which call and gifts for spiritual formation can be explored.

But the truth is, the urge toward relationship is strong enough to transcend even the most mechanical model of centralized efficiency. Our bodies know that we are not machines. Our senses are constantly scanning for input of tastes, sounds, smells, and sights. Our bodies remind us that we are not interchangeable parts of a mechanical universe. We breathe in the air that has been breathed out by our neighbors. We use words because we want to communicate, to join with others. We meet at the level of our humanity long before economics and politics divide us into groups and categories. Human beings are always interacting in a self-correcting system. We are born to belong, to join and meet and connect.

Human groupings also remind us that uniformity is only temporary. Creativity keeps breaking through. Humor harbors another perspective; artists and writers point to another reality. Economic, political, and religious organizations have an organic element because we bring our humanity to the organizational mix. All organizations are self-correcting, even when that capacity is unnoticed and unrewarded. Margaret Wheatley, in her essay "What Is Our Work," describes the havoc that results when a union decides to "work to the rule" instead of doing the many little extras that keep an organization functioning. She notes that people *want* to make things work and have always made personal adjustments to accomplish common tasks. Rejecting the either/or categories of a mechanical worldview, Wheatley draws on the images of interrelatedness in quantum physics to speak about human organization. She suggests that relationship is the basic characteristic of all things.[2]

If this is true, and I believe it is, then call cannot be manifested fully without community. There is no such thing as an "individual" call, even though call enters the world through one person's revelation and risk. Though held and nurtured by one person, a call must quicken response in another and then another. Through call, we are each drawn to leadership and responsibility for the piece of eternity that is ours to tend. As we discover the points of our connection, we also become aware of our interdependence. This allows us to be imperfect, to be fully human instead of some idealized package of goodness or skills. When we discover that our creativity thrives where there is room for giving and receiving help from others, we knowingly participate in the "dance of creation." It is only then that we can begin to experience the fullness of purpose for which we have been created.

• RULER & MAGICIAN •

In myth, Stage Five parallels the final phase of Joseph Campbell's description of the hero's journey, "the return."[3] In their book *King, Warrior, Magician, Lover*, Robert Moore and Doug Gillette describe the archetypes of Ruler and Magician. The Ruler is an insider who seeks harmony and prosperity for the kingdom while the Magician operates outside the system, using alchemy to transform common elements into treasure. The Ruler has an "ordering function" along with a capacity for fertility and blessing for the whole realm. In its fullness, they say, the Ruler archetype brings qualities of reasonable and rational patterning, integration and integrity, stability, centeredness and calm, mediating vitality or life-force in the land and people. All of these are relational qualities directed toward gathering and centering diverse energies. Implied in the Ruler's character is a deep sense of interconnectedness.[4]

In the biblical story, Esther stepped into her fullness as a Ruler when she entered the King's chamber a second time. There was no agonized period of preparation, no resistance or hesitation. Even though her status had not changed, she was ready to claim her relational power. The King acknowledged her right to be there by asking in a brotherly tone, "What is it this time?"

Speaking Ruler-to-Ruler, Esther appealed to the King's desire for a reasonable solution to the dilemma created by his own legal system, which did not allow him to undo one of his own edicts. The King agreed with her suggestion that the Jews be allowed to defend themselves in a one-day war outside the capital and a two-day war inside the capital where, presumably, they would need more time to solidify their safety. The solution, though bloody and violent, seemed to fit the situation they were in—maintaining boundaries and time limits while allowing the political system to reconfigure itself.

Moore and Gillette describe the other archetype, the Magician, as a knower and master of technology, confessor and priest in charge of initiating others into the mysteries of transformation. The Magician, they say, can effectively bless and curse, deflate arrogance in others and stand as a mediating figure between divine and human realms. If the Ruler is a pastoring figure, nurturing and caring for order in the empire, then the Magician is a priestly figure, presiding over transformation, connecting the *kairos* realm of God with the *chronos* world of humans. Both archetypes are needed for a healthy organization.[5]

In the biblical story, Gideon was more Magician than Ruler, although he certainly was the recognized leader when his men went into battle. The elements of surprise and deception in his battle plan suggest that Gideon used more magic than might to accomplish victory over the well-armed Midianites. He broke his three hundred men into companies of one hundred each, armed them with a trumpet, a pitcher, and a candle, and sent them into battle position. These unusual weapons signal that this battle was one of inner transformation. The trumpet is an instrument of call, of awakening and alerting the soul for engagement. Clay jars are common containers for daily life, and the torch is a traditional sign of wisdom and enlightenment.

When the right moment came, all three companies smashed their pots, blew on their trumpets, and raised their torches high as they shouted. And the enemy ran away in disgrace. It was a masterpiece of ingenuity and coordination, of relatedness and call. The army acted as one body, deft and sure of their purpose and mission together.

So successful was the Hebrew army under Gideon's leadership that they chased down the fleeing Midianites and then had to deal with jealous "would-be" warriors who had been sent home or never called in the first place. Such opposition from envious onlookers is a negative aspect of relationships that we often overlook—but the biblical story does not. Call often provokes opposition.

As Gideon dealt with his jealous countrymen, his long story of testing God's call was played out. Even though he refused to become their Ruler, he laid the groundwork for a generation of peace. Gideon mediated God to his people in a way that Esther did not because he was able to take his place in their midst.

• LEADERSHIP •

Leadership in a community of imperfect human beings is exercised differently by a Ruler than by a Magician. Esther led by staying within the confines of law and tradition, using the structures of the Babylonian legal system to confront the misuse of power by Haman and bring relief to her people. As a woman, Esther could not have taken the throne herself, but she embodied the Ruler's style of leadership as fully as any woman could in her time.

Leadership as a Ruler does not mean tyranny, although the shadow side certainly could be that. At its best, the Ruler is concerned about fairness and equity, justice and mercy for those at the margins. In Stage Five, a called Ruler exercises authority on behalf of the whole organism (company, state, school, church) rather than for personal gain. The perspective of call enlarges the Ruler's frame of reference from ego satisfaction to the good of the whole body. Just as Esther's call saved her people from sure extermination, our call will require courage and discernment about what is good for the whole body.

Gideon, on the other hand, used "magic" to accomplish his leadership in community. He and his men won their battle with a "crash and yell" strategy to surprise and disorganize the enemy. This is Magician work—smoke and mirrors to confuse a superior force. Their small force and unorthodox method was a sign of God's mysterious presence. Gideon mediated Spirit to his men, bringing his troops into concerted action by his charisma and spirit power.

As one of the oppressed people, Gideon could not depend upon a system of laws to protect his army. He had to take action that was entrepreneurial and independent, creative and confrontive at the same time. Their weapons would not have been enough even to defend themselves, but their timing, faith, and courage were enough to rout the enemy. Gideon's leadership and charisma drew others into a functioning body, ready to give their lives for the sake of delivering their people from bondage. Gideon's call sustained them all as he performed his transforming function.

In truth, leadership that emerges from call must have qualities of both Ruler and Magician. The danger in assuming the Ruler role is that we will not be able to change our own rules—like the King in Esther's story. The underbelly of the Magician's role is, of course, that we will lose sight of God and think that our powers come from ourselves.

• *FINDING COMMUNITY* •

What we are drawn to can tell us much about the call that is emerging in us, like a seed sprouting when it has the right growing conditions. Among the institutional forms of our culture, religious communities can be a place where we nourish call. In *Meeting Jesus Again for the First Time,* Marcus Borg describes three distinct traditions in Hebrew scripture in which people encounter God.[6] First, there is an EXODUS perspective focused on deliverance from the dominant system following a strong leader like Moses—or Gideon. Secondly, there is an EXILE perspective focused on fellowship and small group support for living a disciplined life in an alien culture, recalling our true home that is somewhere else—as Esther did. Thirdly, there is a PRIESTLY perspective focused on rules and rituals to define membership. Modern churches, Borg suggests, reflect one of these three perspectives in their life and liturgy.

If we need or want deliverance from enslavement, we will be drawn to an EXODUS community, toward a charismatic leader who can lead us toward an alternative reality or, like Gideon, discover that we are called to the task of leadership ourselves. Exodus communities provide an alternative vision from the dominant culture. For members, they are life-giving and often liberating, as African American congregations were during the civil rights era and still are in many inner-city neighborhoods.

If we are not called to escape, but rather to live an alternative vision amid structures created and run by others, we will be drawn to an EXILE community where we can find support for the tough choices that face us in the places where we live and work. Exile communities exist within the dominant culture and depend more on a disciplined inner life and small committed teams, or mission groups, to withstand cultural pressures that would co-opt the loyalties and vision of its members.

Or, if we want a "pure society" of like-minded persons, we may be drawn to a church where the rules are clear, doctrines definitive, and the rituals give us the security of the PRIESTLY strand of faith. Priestly communities focus on activities within the community rather than on interactions with the surrounding world.

At the Seekers Church to which I belong, we have claimed our identity as an EXILE congregation. My husband, Peter, describes the essence of our community with these words:

For a long time I've identified my own life story—and the story of most in Seekers—with the stories of exile, [with] stories of faithful people who were sent by God to labor in institutions they did not create and do not control . . . trying to do justice, love mercy, and walk humbly with God . . . When God's people are living into the Exile Way, they can't change the system . . . but they do have considerable power to create new options or introduce new ideas.[7]

Because Seekers is a community gathered around the call to "be church" together, worship is not a performance we come to critique but an experience of community we come to engage with in the context of God's story. We do not depend upon a professional clergy and have, instead, organized our life around the premise that God is speaking to all of us if we will listen. A mission group writes the liturgy and provides a liturgist to hold the form and tradition, while different people from the congregation preach every week. Altars change with the liturgical seasons; music is varied because we use CDs and tapes instead of having a choir; prayer comes from the congregation instead of a prayer book.

Our primary place of belonging, however, is not the worship service but in small mission groups where we try to stay accountable for an intentional inward journey of prayer, reading, and journal-keeping. Most of our members work in some form of child advocacy and, while our span of influence may be small, the call to be in servant ministry is lively for us. As an EXILE community, these mission groups are not just a way to get work done but a crucible of spiritual formation.

• *CALLED COMMUNITY* •

A "called" community shares a clear purpose, with enough structure and tradition to offer mutual guidance and opportunities to experiment with call and enough commitment to allow the deeper currents of soulwork time to develop. Religious orders have traditionally been the only way to experience a called community, but today small working teams, meditation and retreat centers, and even twelve-step groups function this way. Such a spirit-centered community is much more than an organization with business to conduct efficiently or a task to perform. Spiritual community, wherever it happens, is a place where we practice loving those with whom we do not have much in common—except our common call. We need to remember that the word "religious" comes from the Latin *ligare, to bind or connect.* Religious life is about reconnection with the ligaments that give a community both flexibility and strength. The body image is important to the essence of Stage Five of the soulwork cycle, learning to relate.

Developing a community where most of the people can be operating out of a sense of their call is not easy or particularly orderly. Most of us live with several fragmented communities, patched together by common activity. A more committed community may develop when people share a common professional interest, such as poets who gather to read their work aloud or musicians who play chamber music together.

Entering into community can be a fearful thing for people who have fought hard to achieve independence. The experience of Jesse, a young man at Seekers, comes to mind. As a newcomer, Jesse had attended some of the adult education classes at our School of Christian Living. He got a taste of "covenant community" by exploring a mission group. This is where people often encounter those they would least like to be with. Some become disillusioned and turn away from deeper commitment because they hold an idealized image of what community *ought* to provide. But some embrace the disillusioning process of organic community and stay. An additional commitment to core membership in Seekers is open to anyone who feels called to care for the whole community.

Jesse was in the process of becoming a core member when he wrote this reflection:

Since I made the decision sixteen months ago to come back to Seekers and to make it my primary community of faith, I have found myself drawn into community in new and qualitatively different ways than I have heretofore experienced in my life. I have come to realize that, in my previous experiences of community, I have tended to have one foot in and one foot out. I can see in new ways how my fear of commitment to community stems both from the pain of growing up in a chaotic family of origin as well as the rampant individualism of this culture, which in my own way I have internalized.

Where before it was easy for me to see the places where the community isn't perfect, I now have a much deeper appreciation for the sense of loving bounty and grace. No community is/can be perfect. No community will be the "perfect family" I wish I had growing up. I have had to learn and relearn that, and I am sure I will need to learn it again!

I grew up "holding my cards close to the chest." It was a good survival skill. Lately I have felt called to let my community in, more and more, to where I am in the moment rather than waiting until I feel totally comfortable . . . I am relating in new ways to people within Seekers, and I would say especially to people with whom I would not normally be attracted to being "friends," including people with whom I feel real differences and have otherwise found very easy to avoid. My involvement with the community feels a lot less exclusively about trying to meet my own needs now, and more about trying to live a life of discipleship.

As I began to voice out loud my new sense of commitment to Seekers, I began to immediately feel more invested, and as I began to feel more invested, I started to see areas where I felt called to use my gifts in the service of the community. Specifically, I felt a desire to find a way to share some of the musical energy which has been generated in the last year and a half within the community sing-a-longs . . . Part of the transition for me is learning to be a part of a larger musical pool which feeds the life of the community, rather than being a solo act. Frankly, it is not a totally easy transition for me, and yet, I am excited about what is happening here and look forward to more! [8]

Jesse was quite frank to say that the transition had not been easy. As he let go of his wish for "the perfect family"—and the inevitable disappointment that had kept him away from full commitment—he began to see the sacred even among those he did not like. Much in our culture would have had Jesse stop at Stage Four and keep his call to music at the performance level. Having left his family of origin where he "held his cards close to his chest," Jesse's experience of entering a mission group to offer his musical gifts in worship had other results—especially in terms of relationships. By sharing his gift of writing and performing music, he was able to move to a deeper experience, where his gifts for music could be shaped and spread by the needs of the community. He could relate to and work with people who had gifts and calls different from his own. Instead of being primarily a solo performer, Jesse developed his capacity for cooperation and partnership, stewardship and eldering—Ruler and Magician qualities that make him a valuable member of the wider community.

• BEYOND RELATING •

In Stage Five, we discover our leadership and kinship with others in new ways. We wrestle with the ambiguities of power and opposition. Ethical questions emerge, and we are called to stretch beyond what we have done in the past. This stage can be exciting and fulfilling because we have a community of people with whom to celebrate—and perhaps also to grieve. In this stage we discover the complexity of chosen family where we may feel more bonded than we ever have with our biological families.

When call takes on institutional forms, we may be tempted to see Stage Five as the completion of call. Certainly it provides the most satisfaction and possibility of worldly success. But biblical and archetypal stories suggest there is yet another stage in which we relinquish more obvious forms of power and become the servant of call.

Stage Six: RELEASE

CHAPTER 9

I took the heavy bag of clay from my car and sat on a stone overlooking the creek that ran through the yard at Virginia Medical Center. My friend Michael lay brain-dead inside from a car accident. His brother asked me to make a vessel for his ashes. Jim could not have known that I had clay in the car, but I did. So I sat for maybe two hours, pinching a good-sized urn and thinking about this man who had so blessed my ministry beyond the church. Periodically he would call for no good reason, saying "You came up in my prayers today. How's it going?" And we would talk.

When I finished, I made one last visit to the ICU where he sat in bed with his huge bandaged head like an Olmec totem figure. I wondered if he could still hear, if he were hanging on to life because he didn't know what would happen next, so I told him about the urn. "They'll take your ashes out by your crab pots," I said, "and the clay will dissolve with you into the water." I could think of nothing else to say. "Thank you . . . for being . . . so real."

Completing the cycle of soulwork means integration, endings, and release. In Stage Six we have an opportunity to weave the earlier stages of call into a conceptual framework that transcends the limits of individual accomplishment and opens us to the mysteries of birth and death. How that is achieved is the heart of Stage Six. We can begin to release control of what we have accomplished, knowing that the time is right to step back from the power-point where call has placed us. Stage Six has a dimension of generativity, of giving our call away to others, of looking for opportunities to pass our experiences on or to let go of them so we can start the soulwork cycle all over again. It is the stage of servant leadership.

In Stage Six, we need to leave behind power, proficiency, and prestige, as happens with graduation or retirement. Or we may need to leave behind a structure of servitude that is known and fa-miliar—a dead-end job, an abusive marriage, or even an old image of God. Some people consistently try to short-circuit the cycle, jumping over this last stage because it requires a degree of ser-vanthood for which they are not ready. Others try to skip Stage Six and stay in the relationship stage because it "feels good" and gives them a sense of power and expression.

Whatever organizational structure group has supported our lives in Stage Five, we need to let go of it and open our hands to be led by Spirit into some form of relinquishment in Stage Six.

Release is the stage of rest, of listening for guidance and fol-lowing in trust because we know we have been led by call in ear-lier stages. It is a time of letting go of our illusions, of the little ways we play god in daily life. We can choose relinquishment and rest, sip from the cup of finality—or fight it. Sleep, for many chil-dren, is a little death, and fighting sleep—or any form of rest—is a ritual battle that persists for some. Yet, as we get older, we learn that experiences of loss and vulnerability make rest an essential part of creative work, a vital part of life. We can enjoy things in the present, open ourselves to what is, and learn to release what has been dear—with faith that something else is possible. We learn that we do not own anything. Nothing is permanent.

Usually Stage Six comes upon us unbidden and unwanted, but if we can embrace release, we can be free to enjoy whatever state we find ourselves in. Whether we have come to the end of the cycle of discovering who we are, or what our work is, or what our gifts are, or even to the final phase of approaching death—living into Stage Six frees us from hanging on to the past to live fully in the present moment, as I did when I pinched a pot for Michael's ashes.

Over a lifetime, we have many opportunities to learn the art of letting go, but parenting is probably the most common experience. Every parent is challenged to give their best—and let go of the results! Parents who think they can control how their children will turn out are simply fooling themselves. Parenting as a spiritual discipline can be preparation for other rounds of the soulwork cycle. Even if completion of a cycle is planned for and desired, Stage Six can mean loneliness and loss of direction. It can leave us feeling bereft.

If we have not lived into the prior stages of call, release will be harder. Sometimes we let go grudgingly, prying our fingers loose, one at a time, from control. If we are unwilling or unable to move away from a position of power or control, this last stage of the soulwork cycle can feel like failure or defeat. If we do not have a larger conceptual framework of call or faith, it is more difficult to shift from control to cooperation.

Sometimes Stage Six can stretch into a satisfying plateau, embracing others without effort. The image of a benign patriarch beaming at his doting children is an idealized image some carry. Others tire of the demands that community makes and are ready to move on toward a new call when the time is ripe. More often, however, Stage Six is truncated by the beginning of a new round of the soulwork cycle. As an old cowboy ballad reminds us, "Ya gotta know when to hold and when to fold . . . " Learning when to let go, as well as when to hang on, is the essence of Stage Six. Learning

Stage 6: Release

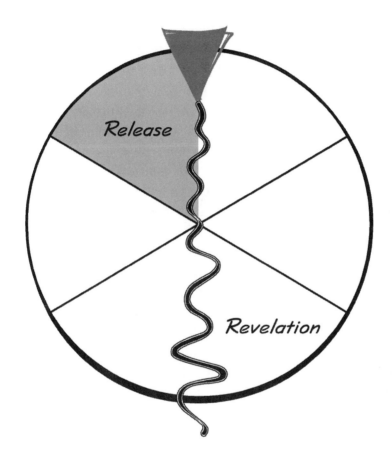

how to love fully and freely without clinging or demanding certain results is the secret of this stage.

• *COUNTERPART OF REVELATION* •

The most important pairing in the soulwork cycle is that of revelation in Stage Three and release in Stage Six. In the third stage, we get a momentary glimpse of the whole picture—what could happen if God's call were lived out to the fullest. When that possibility first comes, we have not done the inner work necessary to trust God for a way through the barriers and obstacles. That vision can be overwhelming and terrifying because there is no way it can be accomplished by one person, and we have not yet found a new community with whom to share the call. But by the time we have come to Stage Six, we have toughened our resolve through risk and learned how to relate our call to other systems, beliefs, and traditions. Soulwork in Stage Six comes from knowing how fully all things are interconnected. We have deepened our trust in the *kairos* realm because we have experienced its nearness and fullness.

In the stories of both Gideon and Esther, the momentary glimpse of divine purpose that each one had in Stage Three came to fruition as their stories ended with a Stage Six experience.

Once Gideon had proved his courage on the battlefield, the people of Israel wanted him to become their King. Gideon wisely declined, saying "I will not rule over you, and my son will not rule over you; the Lord will rule over you." Gideon's response reflected his revelation in Stage Three, when he tore down his father's altar to Baal and declared his allegiance to Yahweh by building a new one. In Stage Six, Gideon embodied the fullness of that earlier revelation when he refused titular leadership. In spite of his victory as a "mighty warrior," Gideon's real lesson was learning to trust the God who promised to go with him. Finally, he could claim the altar named "Peace." During his lifetime, Israel enjoyed peace, but "no sooner had Gideon died than the Israelites again prostrated themselves to Baal" and the cycle began again.

For Esther, the counterpart to Stage Three of her story came when she discovered that she was, indeed, "born for just such a time as this." Although she disappears from our view in the release stage—in a sense, releasing her hold on the story-line—Mordecai claimed the larger, archetypal meaning of her role in his dream: "Haman and I were the dragons, and Esther, the river between."

Mordecai understood that he and Haman represented two warring forces, symbolized by the dragons. The King was simply the framework for their conflict, not the opponent. And Esther, as "the river" that arose from a cry out of the ground and swallowed both dragons, was the agent of God, the power of transformation. Mordecai saw beyond Esther's personal story to God's story of release and deliverance for the Jews. This is an epic drama still celebrated by Jews at Purim today.

Both biblical accounts combine myth and human history to demonstrate human courage and divine guidance—the cycle of call made visible.

• *SAGE & FOOL* •

In myth, Stage Six is characterized by the archetypes of the Sage and the Fool.[1] The Sage is a wisdom figure, seasoned and slow to speak. The Sage may be perceived as a prophet, a healer, or a soothsayer. Also known as a "rainmaker," magician, or sometimes a witch, the Sage exerts spiritual power and presence in a world where that is feared more than favored. Often a storyteller adept at seeing beneath surface appearances, the Sage may live a remote and lonely life, accustomed to simplicity and much silence.

In our culture, we make it hard to claim the role of Sage in Stage Six because we give so much attention to the young who have technological skill and no particular sense of service. We value the productiveness of Stages Four and Five and treat release as failure rather than space for nurturing wisdom. By marginalizing elders and people who have moved out of positions of power in the economic or political realm, we virtually force older men and women toward the archetype of the Fool, at least in public view. Even though there has been some improvement in media presentation of older people, the terrors of Alzheimer's disease and fear of health problems undermine images of eldering Sages.

On the other hand, the Fool brings a child's innocence into the public realm to transform the deadly seriousness that clouds our minds when we pretend to be gods. The Fool is never consistent, never logical or predictable. The Fool makes fun of literal-minded role-players of the world. Instead of putting on make-up and a costume, the Fool reveals our nakedness by unmasking our pretensions with gesture and action. The archetypal Fool lives in the present, mimes with gestures rather than speaking, and does the obvious but socially unacceptable thing. As an outsider, the Fool's comic ways help us accept the limits of our humanity and teach us to laugh and cry with others.

Most of us are afraid of looking foolish, and yet we know the wonderful gift of laughter and storytelling at the end of a hard day or when we need to release stress and relax. The Fool in Stage Six is not a buffoon who does not know any better, but one who reflects and reminds us of human limits.

In the final stage of his soulwork cycle, Gideon provides a classic example of the Fool's role in release, reminding us of how easily we are seduced by power. After his victory, he collected golden earrings from the conquered tribes and melted them into a golden loincloth. Scripture says, "It became a snare to Gideon and his family." Greed and hubris betrayed Gideon's shadow side, revealing his limitations as a leader. While we might be tempted to blame God for calling such a faulty man, this detail gives us a glimpse of how the image of God in this story is big enough to embrace the shadow side of Gideon and his family. Not only was Gideon able to withstand the temptation to become the first King of the Jews, but God was willing to accept Gideon's human failures and bless him with peace and progeny anyway.

In Esther's story, Mordecai became something of a Sage when he recognized his own culpability as one of the two dragons in his dream. He seems to have developed more perspective on his own ambitions. The Greek version of the story, which is the only version to include this dream, probably reveals the patriarchal bias of Scripture, unable to honor Esther as the wise woman she obviously was. Nevertheless, I am struck by the realism in both stories. Both Gideon and Esther become faithful, if flawed, partners in God's plan. Neither is idealized or perfected beyond human recognition.

In this last stage of the soulwork cycle, our idealism is tempered by the reality of human beings doing the best they can, given the resources they have. We choose connection over perfection because we see a bigger picture and a longer time frame. This allows us to embrace life fully where and how we are so we can find a measure of satisfaction in saying "I did what I could" each time we come to this point on the spiral journey.

• *SERVANT LEARNING* •

In Christian mythology, paradoxically, one becomes a Sage by taking on the foolishness of God—that is, the servant role. With the sense of a wisdom teacher, Paul writes to the church at Corinth, "What seems to be God's foolishness is wiser than men's wisdom and what seems to be God's weakness is stronger than men's strength"[2] He was referring to the marginal nature of Jesus' ministry and how, after his death, the Christ-Spirit came to lowly and high-born alike. Jesus' nonhierarchical life and ignominious death provided a mysterious merger of Sage and Fool, and his followers released a new kind of spiritual power into the world even as they struggled to find their own call once he was gone in person. They served a larger purpose than their culture provided, and with their "servant learning," changed the world around them.

Recently, the servant ideas of Robert Greenleaf have surfaced again because they express a deep truth about the nature of leadership over time. Greenleaf spent forty years as an executive with AT&T. Following his retirement in 1964, he published a famous essay, "The Servant as Leader," and spent another twenty-five years as an author, teacher, and consultant until he died in 1990. As he wrote about issues of power and authority, Greenleaf held up a less coercive and more inclusive model than the leadership roles taught in business schools around the country. He focused on those who were already in positions of leadership, inviting them to adopt an ethic of service.[3]

Today Greenleaf's model is being promoted by organizational consultants Ken Blanchard, Stephen Covey, Peter Block, Margaret Wheatley, and others.[4] They describe servant leadership as leadership based on listening more than giving orders. It is a conscious choice to be less than we can be so others can learn to be more than they have been. In truth, in any healthy community—whether family, work team, or church—those who serve as "the glue" of community are usually practicing some form of servant leadership. They put the good of the whole group ahead of what is convenient or most efficient for themselves.

Although Greenleaf said that one must be a servant before becoming a leader, I suspect that we must develop these capacities together, tempering the egocentric focus of our culture with the mystical experience of listening to the voice of God within. While "servant leadership" has become a positive value for those in high-profile jobs, I prefer the term "servant learning" to describe the energy of Stage Six because it suggests the attitude of alertness and receptivity needed for living our call. "Servant learning" happens when we make the shift away from doing it ourselves to helping others listen for their own call.

Only in Stage Six is servant learning truly possible. Serving becomes the natural result of earlier stages of call. There is a freedom and humility in Stage Six that cannot come earlier because we have been ego-involved in the action demanded by our call. It is only in the last stage of the soulwork cycle that the ego thrill of giving and getting can soften to embrace the needs of others. Stage Six is a time to step back from obvious leadership and guide "from the third row back" so others can practice their upfront skills. As we loosen our hold on the responsibilities of leadership and teamwork, we can begin to notice others at the edge, becoming aware of those who do not belong so easily. We can begin to give away what we have achieved, blessing others in the process.

• *GENERATIVITY OR DESPAIR?* •

Some would deny that release is necessary, claiming that we can go from one public success to the next if only we are smart enough. But as we become aware of a deeper sense of call, clinging to success becomes another effort to stop the flow of life in all its complexity. The larger rhythms of life tell us that death and endings are essential. Just as death is a fact of life, so too is release a requirement of call. Every primary focus comes to an end, leaving us with a hiatus, which Erik Erikson described in older people as the choice between generativity or stagnation.[5] If we cannot release a completed cycle and embrace a new call, despair lurks in the shadows. Generativity means embracing change, because we know nothing is permanent. Completing the soulwork cycle brings us to the choice between creativity and stagnation, even at the age of thirty or forty.

Generativity is expressed when we can move into Stage Six with care and concern for others, ready to pass on what we have learned and make space for others to learn in their own way, make their own mistakes, and face the consequences of their actions. Despair arrives when we cannot see a larger framework for these endings and give up the invitation toward new life as we come to the end of what has been challenging and fulfilling before. Whether we choose generativity or despair depends upon us—and grace.

Being generative does not mean we deny the reality of cruelty, evil, or other kinds of exploitation. To those who believe that we create our own reality and can transcend the ravages of time or illness with the "right" belief, the Judeo-Christian story provides a counter message because it is firmly rooted in the *limits* of our flesh as a fact of our humanity. When Jesus was tempted to avoid death by jumping off the Temple spire and letting the angels catch him, he refused. He would not trade his humanity for the tempting fantasy of miraculous rescue. He chose into his mortality—and we can, too.

Endings have a purpose. Limits heighten our sense of risk and adventure. Generativity is a choice in the face of those limits. We can love even if results are not permanent. We can give generously to others even if there is no reward other than what we feel when we do it. *Chronos* time has real value after all. And if we embrace the process of sorting, valuing, and discarding in Stage Six, we can begin to clear space for the next round of call.

Struggle, too, seems part of this final stage. Continuing to create, to give, and to bless takes effort. Those who see spirituality as a blissful state of union with nature overlook the terror, the struggle to survive, the constant threat of death that is part of nature. As one observer said, "People who romanticize nature must not watch the Discovery channel." The wise ones know that all things come to an end. Some develop this capacity through direct experience with death and dying; others develop this capacity by being intentional about the inner dimension of daily life, by practicing, observing, accepting, and releasing as naturally as the way they breathe.

In Stage Six, we loosen our hold on success and exchange the temptations of power to serve the well-being of creation. Wisdom replaces coercive force. Call becomes a trust that God is bigger than any particular part that we have accomplished. We open ourselves to an unknown future and begin to see weakness as part of our strength. Stage Six is not some esoteric skill for the spiritually advanced, but the homely work of learning our humble place in the larger scheme of things.

• *AWARENESS & DETACHMENT* •

Release reminds us that we live in a changing world where things and people die, and newness is constantly born. Without release, we would be tempted to solidify and even idolize what we have initiated. That is the problem with many institutional structures that were highly functional in their inception but ossify over time.

In this sixth stage, we must practice *both* awareness and detachment to let go of the structures we have created, with as much grace as possible. Awareness speaks of consciousness. Detachment requires discipline. In Stage Six, as in the earlier passage between private spirituality and more public expression, detachment becomes a gift. We can love something deeply and still let go.

After living through the whole cycle of call, the Innocent of Stage One has given up his specialness, and the Orphan, her separateness. The Innocent has learned the capacity and perspective for accepting human limitations, and the Orphan knows how to laugh at herself. Instead of blaming others for faults and failures, we have learned acceptance with some ease and good humor. In this stage Buddhist teachings about breathing and smiling make sense, not as some special gift for the super-spiritual but as a simple recognition that we are both common and special, gifted and ordinary. Developing our capacity to live in the present moment and not hang on to the past, however painful or glorious, is a spiritual practice that opens us to the *kairos* realm of God's abiding presence. Conscious practice of release can, in fact, develop the qualities of wider perspective needed for genuine cooperation and teamwork. It is the essence of centering prayer.

In a sermon he gave for Seekers, Ron Arms invites us to understand breathing as a discipline of release:

> *One thing breathing has taught me is the importance of slowing down. There is a saying, "A wise person is never in a hurry." I too often rush through my days, as though there were a reward for getting to the grave first. But watching my breath come in and go out reminds me it is better to do nothing than to waste time.*[6]

Ron's words suggest that breathing is a practice of awareness and detachment *at the same time*. Although useful throughout the cycle of call, conscious attention to the in-and-out movement of one's breath can be a reminder of the dynamic energy of body and spirit merging.

Conscious breathing can help us release the grip of ego and control in Stage Five and serve as a reminder of our freedom to begin again. Noticing where our breath changes direction is a reminder that nothing stays forever, change is inevitable, and we have the freedom to release what has been life-giving in the past—as simply as we can breathe out. Stage Six requires both awareness and detachment, intentionality and attention to the ongoing flow of God's creativity beyond our individual lives and the systems we have created. If we question whether we have done something with awareness, we need to notice how we feel afterward. Attention and awareness enable us to end up refreshed and content—the mark of integrating call.

• *RELEASE & THE SPIRAL JOURNEY* •

Each time we come around to Stage Six in the soulwork cycle, this stage has a special poignancy as we release what has been life-giving in the previous stages and prepare ourselves for a new call.

First Round:
Releasing "Who I am" to find "What my work is."

If we are completing the soulwork cycle for the first time—usually between the ages of twenty and thirty-five—Stage Six demands that we let go of some piece of our hard-won personal identity. Today, identity as an adult is likely to be found in the workplace. Release in Stage Six of the first round of call often comes as we face some instance of betrayal or conflict between our personal ideals and an institution's goals. Young parents often struggle to maintain their former identity as singular adults even as a child changes their work and, hopefully, their call in the world. In earlier generations, having children was the sign of establishing an adult identity—and that still may be the unconscious drive behind many teen pregnancies. However, since the early sixties when "the pill" became widely available, reproduction is not the sign of "being somebody" in the world that it once was. Both men and women sacrifice some elements of their uniqueness and autonomy in Stage Six in what can feel like a loss of soul. It can be lonely and depressing, especially if we are letting go of an established perception of who we are in the world for an unknown future identity that is more relational. Though release is a call to servant learning, it often feels like death!

My friend Carlisle graduated with honors from Yale and completed two years in Costa Rica with a religious mission. She fully expected to be accepted for candidacy as an Episcopal priest, but the Committee on Ministry in her local church refused to endorse her and she was devastated. She had opposed her family to pursue this dream, and now it seemed as if everyone, even God, had abandoned her. When she came to talk with me, she was in shock, as though her sense of self had been destroyed.

With the help of a spiritual director, a job in international development, and several retreats, she has shifted her focus to listening for a new call in the area of international affairs. In this movement from Stage Six of the first round of her soulwork cycle to the beginning of a second round, she opens to the question of *"What is my work?"*

Second Round:
Releasing "What my work is" to find "What my gift is."
At the end of the second round of the soulwork cycle—usually between the ages of thirty-five and fifty—release means letting go of the work we have claimed as "ours." Because the work we have discovered in this period has usually meant a vital shift from "job" to a deeper work, releasing that work feels dangerous. It often means a career change or shift in relationships at home. Whether the shift into Stage Six is caused by internal restlessness or external trauma is not as important as how we deal with it. What is required

is that we step back from our work and see it as part, but not all, of who we are and what we are here for. In this round, Stage Six means learning that work is not the full picture of God's call for us!

People who write about spirituality in the workplace note the consuming nature of work today. Laptop computers, fax machines, cell phones, and beepers mean that we are never outside the range of office demands. The very flexibility that promised to let people tend relationships and work from home has made it more and more difficult to put boundaries around work, particularly if we see our work as "a calling." Release in this second round of call may require that we practice more "Sabbath sense," as author Donna Schaper puts it.[7] Not just a matter of setting aside time for worship, her description of "Sabbath sense" includes disrupting the hold work has on us, paying attention to dreams, keeping a journal, reflecting on Scripture, reading, talking with friends, walking with a prayer mantra . . . whatever helps us stay open to a wider sense of God's timing and direction beyond the consuming nature of our call to our work.

I think of Bill, who was a part-time youth minister and part-time music minister at a Baptist Church. The position had been a good fit for his talents and call to ministry. When the church decided they could not afford him any more and eliminated the job, Bill felt trapped and angry, not ready for the release of Stage Six. With a wife, two children, and year to go on his house lease, Bill signed up with a temp agency, hoping to use his computer skills while he looked for a position with some religious organization whose values he could support. Leaving his church position and competing for a job in the marketplace with skills he did not value highly left Bill feeling like a failure.

Meanwhile, at Faith At Work, I had been without an office person for three months and was desperate to find someone who would see that job as ministry, not just as an office-manager position. To describe that quality in a classified ad seemed impossible, and the people I had interviewed did not seem to value building relationships while doing the work that needed to be done. It happened that Bill's first placement as a temp was with an organizational development firm on the same floor as the Faith At Work office. When the owner of the firm learned of Bill's church background, she came down the hall and, with a look of glee, said, "I think God delivered a letter meant for you to my address."

Stage Six can have a serendipitous quality that we cannot force or control, but for this to happen, we need to be open to a larger picture of our lives than we might have previously held. Both Bill and I had to let go of the traditional answer to the question, "What is my work in the world?" I had to be open to a working partnership instead of the secretarial help I had been looking for, and Bill had to be willing to release his idea of call as being limited to the church.

Third Round:
Releasing "What my gift is" to find "What my legacy is."
If we are completing our third round of the soulwork cycle, somewhere between the ages of fifty and sixty-five, we must let go of defining ourselves in terms of what we have to offer. Beyond work, beyond skills, and finally even, beyond our gifts, Stage Six begins to move us toward the value of unclaimed parts of ourselves. As we live into the Sage or Fool archetypes, we may discover unsuspected resources that God calls forth in the last round of call.

Letting go in this round of call can introduce the mystical expansiveness of *kairos* time. For me, this experience of release came when Peter and I had the opportunity to spend a month in Vietnam. In 1995, through a friend on the Faith At Work Board, we had hosted two Vietnamese doctors in our home and learned that one of them had been born in Duc Pho where Peter had lived thirty years before. During the Vietnam War, Peter had served as a District Advisor with the U.S. Army, trying to keep minimal governmental services going in an isolated village south of the DMZ, with two other Americans and thousands of Vietnamese refugees to house. "Come and visit us in Vietnam," the doctors had said warmly, "and we'll go back to Duc Pho together."

A year later, we flew to Hanoi and spent a week getting accli-
mated. Peter practiced his language capability and shed the layer
of fear and self-protection that emerged when we landed . . . the war
was still close in his psyche, we learned. One night, walking down a
dark street back to the little hotel where we were staying, he
stopped and took a deep breath. "Ah. I've got it. No one's stalking
us!" It had taken several days of walking, talking, eating, feeling
the normality of people on the city streets to reach this level of
body-knowing.

Then we flew to Quang Ngai, where Dr. A hosted us. For a
week we were taken around the countryside where Peter had lived.
On the last night, Dr. A entertained us at his home instead of the
usual restaurant meals we had shared with officials. Toward the
end of the meal, talk turned to the war years. When questioned
about his work in Duc Pho, Peter took a deep breath, and said,
"Your guys used us for target practice in the village before they
took on the American troops. I still remember seeing a wanted
poster with my picture on it."

The group of men and women around the table nodded and
murmured among themselves. Then Dr. A replied soberly, "I was
thirty miles away, over there in the mountains, digging bullets out
of our troops with no water and no lights." Then he looked at both
of us, reached his hand across the table and said quietly, "We are
both lucky to be alive. Let us build peace together."

Years fell away. In his gesture, the curtain opened, and I saw
the realm of God as we sat at table together, sharing food and drink.
It was true communion and healing we had not expected . . . release
from bonds we had not even been aware of . . . God's gift.

In the third round of call, release can come in this surprising
way. We may be conscious of certain gifts and quite unconscious of
others. For thirty years, both Peter and I had pursued a conscious
spiritual path that had deepened and widened our capacity to hold
the complexity of love and forgiveness. Even then, we did not expect such grace and healing as we both felt that evening in Vietnam.

Fourth Round:
Releasing "What my legacy is."

For all of us, release in the fourth round of the soulwork cycle brings a sense of call to our dying. Stage Six of this round will surely test whether we have done our inner work in earlier rounds. If we are fortunate, there will be time to create something out of our dying process. Elizabeth O'Connor, whose books about The Church of the Saviour inspired so many to new forms of commitment and awareness of call, wrote this letter to the wider community about her dying process:

> *You, dear friends, have known every step of the way what I have needed. You have kept my heart in peace. Each morning and night I thank God for your prayers and my healing. This is important to me. It gathers you around a communion table spread out in my heart. It little matters if the healing for which I give thanks is a healing into life or a healing into death. In me is a deep knowing that a part of you will go with me where I go, and where you are I will be. Such is the eternal nature of the love we have in God. It knows no boundaries of here and there.*[8]

Not many will be as conscious of their release stage as Elizabeth O'Connor was, but others will be touched and expanded when we live fully into dying, as people such as Elizabeth Kubler Ross and those involved in hospice care have helped so many do.

• *BEYOND RELEASE* •

The process of release in Stage Six is made easier if we have stories and rituals and examples of others to follow. A church community, for example, can help enormously with its sacraments and central story of death and resurrection. The ritual of communion or

Eucharist touches the unconscious levels of our being where arche-type and shadow live, reminding us that death is not the end of the story. Knowing that we have made a contribution to the larger col-lective of ongoing life can be a sustaining image when we let go of security we loved or hated. Community ritual holds the story, giv-ing us space, time, and context for our feelings of loss and joy at having others to receive what we have to give.

Even in our final round of the soulwork cycle, the spiral jour-ney is not finished. Each person's life is one part of the ongoing creation. Release always requires some new form of being. I think of those who gathered around Elizabeth O'Connor in her last year. Even as she let go, we began a new round of call without her pres-ence—but with her spirit among us.

The soulwork cycle is not a linear path from youth to death but rather a spiral inward and outward, joining body and spirit more intimately on the soul-full path. A sense of completion in Stage Six will always give way to the chaos of Stage One as we begin the journey again at a different level, living out the sacred story of life on this planet with as much consciousness and discernment as we can embody. The invitation is always there to begin again.

Headwaters

CHAPTER 10

On a high rocky cliff reached by a trail that is frequently blocked by landslides, Triple Divide Creek begins as a trickle. Within sight, the spring-fed waters begin to flow north toward the Arctic Ocean, west toward the Columbia River and on to the Pacific, and east to the Missouri and Mississippi Rivers, which empty into the Caribbean and the Atlantic. On the flat rocky ground, thick with moss and blueberry bushes, it is easy to step across the clear gurgling rivulets without noticing which one we have crossed. I wonder which way I am going?

A t the point where the last stage of the soulwork cycle touches the first stage of the next round, trickling headwaters mark the passage between the three public stages at the end of one soulwork cycle and the more private stages at the beginning of a new cycle, where a new call must incubate inside once again.

The transit between the release stage of one cycle and the re-sist stage of the next can be almost invisible. We may hardly notice the headwaters of what later becomes the great dividing river be-tween public action and personal spirituality. And the more deeply we have lived into the open-handed stance of the release stage, the more subtle our resistance is likely to be as we move into the first stage of a new cycle. But if we do not cross the headwaters of call into a new round of the soulwork cycle, we will tend to stay frozen in one form, resisting the notion of call as Gideon and Esther each did at the beginning of their stories.

• *SPIRITUAL HUNGER* •

Which way shall we go? What direction will the next round be? What is God's next call to the soul?

In earlier times, someone "in authority" provided answers to the key questions of soulwork: *Who am I? What is my work? What is my gift? What is my legacy?* Builders (born before 1929) and Bridgers (born before 1945) grew up within a largely unconscious commu-nity network of relationships to support their individual aspira-tions. They expected an authority figure such as the church to ask spiritual questions and provide the answers. Government cooper-ated by supporting church activities and keeping businesses closed on Sunday. Unaccustomed to the inward terrain of spiritual search, Builders and Bridgers will need encouragement to cross the headwaters of call into the personal challenge of the first three stages of a new call. For them, learning to leave the public realm of institutional answers and pay attention to the "still, small voice" inside is the challenge.

For those who came to adulthood after 1963, just the opposite is true. Boomers and Busters are more familiar with the private and personal side of spiritual questions and less comfortable with organized religion. Stanley Hauerwas and Will Willimon suggest

Headwaters

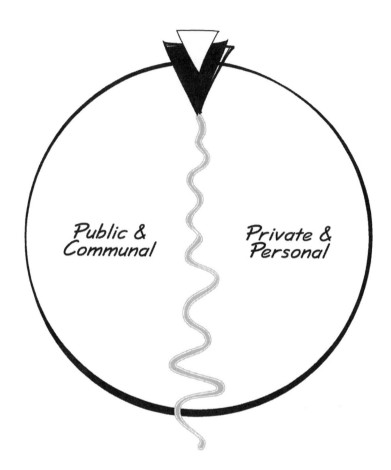

in their book *Resident Aliens* that 1963 was a spiritual watershed in American life.[1] Kennedy's assassination marked the beginning of public unrest as civil rights and anti-Vietnam activists took to the streets. As the postwar generation reached early adulthood and the Information Age took hold of our public life, old certainties were replaced by new questions. Since then, Americans have experienced a fundamental change in their search for meaning and purpose in life. Old authorities have lost their hold on our imagination. As church attendance began to drop and individuals began to search beyond traditional answers to their spiritual questions, we entered the post-Christian age.

Boomers (born before 1946) and Busters (born before 1965) are more suspicious of public institutions and packaged answers, more at home with the spirituality of the first three stages of call. Many have no religious tradition to draw on and do not bring the coherence of tradition into their search for call. For them, the challenge is to join together the inward and outward aspects of call. They will have to rediscover ways of being in community.

Younger people especially have grown up without a mythical framework of biblical stories or trustworthy church communities. Satellite communication makes it possible to hear and see spiritual teachers from many traditions and to pursue "spirituality" without the context of community relationships. More and more people are seeking guidance for the personal aspects of call—resist, reclaim, and revelation—by going on retreat, seeking spiritual direction, going on vision quests, joining meditation groups, purchasing self-help books, and attending conferences where they can sample a rich array of spiritual teachers.

I believe this spiritual hunger is a sign of the Spirit calling us to new forms and deeper attention to the presence of God in our daily lives. It is no coincidence that we have these guides coming into our collective consciousness at the very time when institutional answers no longer serve. Resources are becoming available, trickling into the marketplace, refreshing those who dare to drink at clear bubbling headwaters and consider the possibility of call to new life, no matter which round of call we are struggling with.

The danger is that we will try to do it alone, without community, without those ritual reminders that we are not gods. Churches still provide a place where the stories of call are told and sung, where community forms around particular calls, and where God's larger vision of shalom and reconciliation is celebrated week after week.

Parts of the journey *will* have to be traversed alone, but we will always need the support and challenge of a larger community to complete the cycle. Most of us will resist alone in Stage One but reclaim together in Stage Two. We may experience the third stage of revelation alone and then depend on another for help with crossing the Poison River. On the more public side of the soulwork cycle, we may risk some new endeavor alone or with a partner in Stage Four, then seek a community where call can be embedded in a new "culture" of relating in Stage Five, with its rituals and roles. Finally, the sixth stage of release is likely to be a lonely journey of relinquishment within a social context—if we are being generative rather than withdrawn and hopeless.

As we cross the headwaters of call, there will be times when we are not at all sure we are on the right track. Release gets mixed up with resist. We may retrace our steps more than once. A thousand distractions will crop up, but at this point in the cycle, new call comes like birdsong in the night: simple, impossible, and persistent.

• *BEGINNING AGAIN* •

In my own life, this sense of crossing the Headwaters of call into a new stage happened while Peter and I were still in Vietnam. Even though Vietnam is a Communist country and religion is officially banned, I knew that the exiled peace activist monk, Thich Nhat Hahn, might still have followers in Hue, the old imperial capital just north of Quang Ngai where we had been visiting. I hoped we might find some of evidence of their influence there.

We visited several temples where the guidebook said peace demonstrations had taken place, but we found no evidence of a living community. Then, after visiting a couple of royal tombs, we stopped at Tien Mu, a temple often featured as the icon of Hue. First, we noticed there was no ticket-taker at the gate. Other temples had been turned into tourist attractions, but this one seemed to be a working temple. Then we noticed monks in their gray habits working in the garden—another sign that this was not the government-sanctioned order of mendicants. Walking further, we saw a vintage Austin car displayed in an open garage with a small description in English: this car had taken a monk to Saigon in 1963, where he immolated himself in public to protest the war. This clue tugged at my soul.

Turning away from the car, I noticed a sliding screen that was partially open and a small sign saying this area was closed to tourists. Knowing then it was a holy place, I saw beyond the door a small statue of the Buddha and, without thinking, I made a prayerful gesture with my hands and bowed. We walked on with a small group of visitors, but when we returned to the same spot, a smiling monk stood there and said to me in perfectly good English, "I saw you bow. Won't you come and have tea with me?" So Peter and I stepped away from the group and went into the room where, it turns out, this monk lived.

Did he know of Thich Nhat Hahn?

"Yes, he was my teacher's teacher." As the monk poured tea, we learned this his own teacher had been in jail for many years, that he was the senior monk, and that there were twelve others living there. He proudly mentioned that two novices had joined them in the past year. It seemed like a woefully small group, but the community was clearly alive.

As a young man, he had been a social work student in Saigon during the war, where he had learned English. He showed us the only collection of books that we saw while we were in Vietnam. I asked if I could take his picture. Yes, he was happy to put on his bright yellow robe and let me do that. When I asked if I could send him a copy of the photograph, he said, "Perhaps you could let Thich Nhat Hahn know that we are well here." Then he added, "The government censors our mail and has confiscated our radio, so we must depend upon people like you to remind us that God has not forgotten us."

In that moment, just as in the healing moment at Dr. A's table, the curtain between this world and the next opened for an instant.

Just as our connection with the former "enemy" in Quang Ngai had scrubbed old war wounds clean, the "chance" encounter with this monk in Hue gave me a glimpse of God's call to a world community that would take me into the next round of ministry.

• *SPIRAL PATH* •

The image of this spiraling journey is like a path circling downward, toward greater focus and clarity about why we are alive. We return periodically to the bare ridge between Stage Six and Stage One of the next round. It is a place to see how far we have come, to catch our breath, to notice the next round, to feel the restless tug of call. To move on, we must turn our backs on the view, lower ourselves down off the ledge, and head back into the underbrush. We know there is more inner work to do, traversing the stages of resist, reclaim, and revelation from another entry point, until we come to the Poison River once again.

Each time we cross the Poison River, there will be more to do and others with whom to share it. Completing each cycle of call will mean claiming our soulwork in the public realm of institutions where we risk, build relationships around our sense of call, and release once again. When we understand that the soulwork cycle takes place within a larger spiral journey that is open-ended, we can truly embrace the *kairos* dimension of our lives and stay centered in our relationship with the cosmic creation story.

• • •

• • •

As I wrote at the outset of this book, each time we progress through the six stages of call, we learn more about how to listen for a new call. Experience with previous call may not make it easier to say "yes" to a new call, but each journey through the stages of call builds the qualities of soul necessary for the next round. Once again, I invite you to return to this simple practice:

Sit quietly and focus on your breathing,
counting from one through four and then return to one,
while your mind rests with the question,
"What is my call now?"

• • •

A Soulwork Cycle Retreat

A s I wrote in the Introduction, my hope is that you will share your reflections on this book with other people: *"Knowing that there is a pattern and progression to call can be encouraging when we feel lost and alone . . . knowing where we are in each cycle can offer comfort, companionship, and guidance in an otherwise lonely journey."*

I invite you to consider using the Soulwork Cycle as a basis for a weekend retreat for a group or church. The design format that I have included here is one that we have developed over a twenty-year period in my work with Faith At Work. It is not dependent upon bringing in an outside "specialist." In fact, the design specifically encourages local leadership, with one person functioning as a "mentor" for the team.

The flow of this design will help you create enough safety and stimulation in the microcosm of a weekend event so that people can experience the liberating power of soulwork. And because it does not encourage dependence upon "the leaders," the design allows both the participants *and* the leadership team to listen for God's call in whatever age and stage they find themselves.

• TEAM LEADERSHIP •

You will need a leadership team of three or four individuals to share in the preparation and coordination of this retreat. Ideally, one person with some retreat experience and an overall sense of the design's purpose will serve as the mentor. The other members of the team should be selected to include a variety of ages, work, and marital experience, as well as special gifts that each person might contribute to the event, such as hospitality, music, and a vision for providing this experience. It is also important that the team members have done enough "inner work" to avoid spiritual exhibitionism.

In addition to going over the design and planning "who is going to do what," it is important that your leadership team schedule time ahead of the event to get together and share where each of you are on your soulwork journey. This will give you a sense of operating as a single body, not as separate individuals. This preparation will serve as the "doorway" into your event. I think you will find that once retreat participants become engaged in the process, they will "carry" the event themselves.

• SOME BASICS •

While this design is formatted for a "traditional" weekend retreat, beginning on Friday evening and ending on Sunday, you can certainly modify the form to fit your particular needs. You may need to "compress" the design to fit your time frame. You may want to consider using sequential segments of the retreat design as a weekly group meeting. The important point to remember is that this is more about experience than information. Be sure to allow enough time for people to write their responses to questions and to share some of those with a small group.

When you are planning your retreat, think about the number of participants you might have. From my experience in leading weekend retreats, I think a group between 16 and 30 participants is ideal because participants can relate to the whole circle as well as their smaller groups. You want to have enough people present for diversity and not so many that people will "get lost" in the crowd.

When you think about announcing your retreat, make your flyer or brochure a supplement to *personal* invitations. When you do prepare information, make sure that you let people know that this will be an experiential and relational event that may involve art and movement, as well as more traditional forms of spiritual search, such as prayer, silence, and creative worship. Regardless of whether your retreat is at held on a secluded retreat grounds or in a church basement, it is important to prepare the room before the first participants arrive. This may include setting chairs in a circle, creating an "altar" on the floor in the center with a candle, flowers, open Bible, and other elements relating to the theme. Make the room as welcoming as possible. Provide the information participants need, including a time schedule for the weekend. Have name tags ready and registration information available for "new arrivals," if that is appropriate.

• *FRIDAY EVENING* •

7:00 to 8:45 P.M.
GETTING STARTED

7:00   As you begin the retreat, keep the concept of *safety* in mind. People will not risk a deeper encounter unless they feel safe enough to extend themselves. Start with a welcome by the leadership team mentor that includes a few words about the purpose of the retreat. Describe briefly the concept of "leadership by a team and not just one person." Offer a prayer to invite people to intentional awareness of God's presence.

7:15   A good way to start is to let people name themselves into the circle. If possible, given the size of the group and the time you have for your event, go around the circle and have each person say his/her name and ask the group to respond with, "Welcome [*insert each person's name*]" It is important for each person to listen to others, as well as to speak for themselves, from the very beginning.

7:45   Then move to some "mixer" questions to initiate interaction among the participants. The person from your leadership team who leads this portion should be centered and inviting. It is important that the directions are clear and that the participants know how much time they have to answer each question.

The questions you choose for the mixers should follow a progression from simple past events (e.g., "Where were you born? Where did you live when you started school? What was your favorite childhood game?, etc.) to questions that are a little deeper, related to the theme of the event, such as:

• Recall how you felt about leaving home the first time.
• When have you felt led to make a major change in your life?
• If you were in trouble, who would you call for help?

For each question, ask people to mill about the room and choose one person with whom to share their answer. I suggest allowing two minutes for each question. This gives each person one minute to talk, which invites more than a "yes" or "no" answer but does not allow *too* much time. It is helpful to have a chime or some musical sound to indicate when "time is up" for each person. After the second chime, when both people have responded, suggest that each person take a deep breath, look carefully at their partner, and remember what they have heard or said. Then proceed with the next mixer question, asking people to mill about again and choose a different person to share their answers with each time. Usually 4 or 5 "simple" mixer questions will be enough to shift the energy in the room toward participation rather than observation. Adding 2 or 3 questions that go a little deeper will give people a chance to begin connecting with a few people in the room.

8:15   An important part of this retreat design is that people will be working with a smaller group of people within the larger group framework. Depending on your numbers, a four-person group is ideal. Prepare participants for this by describing the process. Let them know that they will be choosing into a group with whom they will be spending time over the course of the retreat. Let the guidelines for this process come from the entire group. For example, you might ask participants, "What helps you feel received by others in a small group?" and list the responses on newsprint. Limit the list to six or eight items. Be sure your list includes:

- confidentiality
- no advice
- share time equally

One of the easiest ways I have seen to facilitate the formation of small groups is to ask people first to choose a partner. It is important that they not choose a good friend, roommate, or spouse because that would give a special advantage to that pair within a foursome. I usually give the first pair a chance to connect with another mixer question. Then ask each pair of partners to choose another pair to make a foursome (Quad). (If you have an uneven number and want to keep most groups in Quads, ask an outgoing person to step aside and then choose into a pair, making one Triad among the Quads.) Have Quads get acquainted by sharing anything they would like to say in one minute each. (Use the chime to make sure they keep this contained.) The leadership team will form a Quad of their own in order to be supportive of each other in this shared leadership model.

8:45   BREAK

9:00 to 10:00 P.M.
Stage One: RESIST

9:00   After a short break, call the participants together with music. Keep it simple, something everyone can sing without books. It is helpful if you write the words on newsprint ahead of time.

The mentor from the leadership team should then introduce the theme for the retreat. You might want to hand out preprinted copies of the soulwork cycle (see page 39) and the stories of Gideon and Esther (from Chapter Two). "Tell" the portion of each biblical story that portrays the first stage of RESISTANCE. You might also want to provide background material, such as historical setting, scenario, characters, etc. Then relate the biblical story to the theme of RESISTANCE and tell some part of your own story that illustrates this stage.

This fundamental element of personal sharing, or "modeling," from the leadership team runs throughout this retreat design, This kind of public sharing from the team models for participants how they might do the same when they move into their small groups.

9:20   To conclude the evening, have a pre-planned question for journaling or discussion written on newsprint ahead of time. (For example, *"What am I resisting in my life?"*) Give participants about 10 minutes to answer this question privately, providing silence or a quiet musical background for their journaling or contemplation. (I have found that when people have this private time, they are more inclined to stick to their own experience and go deeper in their verbal sharing with a small group.)

Then invite participants to gather with their newly formed small group and spend 20 minutes sharing their responses.

You might want to close your evening with singing or prayer or some movement. It is important to close on time, as a way of honoring boundaries. If you begin and end each session on time, people will respond because they know what to expect.

• *SATURDAY* •

Before breakfast, I like to offer a time of meditation and quietness together for those who want to come early. Fewer people will come to this optional activity, so arrange chairs or pillows in a circle, light a candle to signal the beginning of this quiet period, and be there yourself, sitting quietly, holding the space with your presence.

You can vary this with some gentle stretching. Another option is to encourage silence until breakfast and suggest that people to work with their journals around the theme of resistance.

9:00 to 10:15 A.M.
Stage Two: RECLAIM

9:00   Begin with some stretching together, sing one or two songs, and end this coming together with some kind of centering prayer.

9:15   Another leadership team member (someone other than the previous evening's presenter) should introduce Stage Two of the soulwork cycle, RECLAIM, using the biblical stories of Gideon and Esther. Whoever is doing this input should have read the chapter carefully and picked out some of the subheadings that seem particularly important in his/her own experience of discovering lost or disowned parts of the self. I often use a diagram of concentric circles on a newsprint sheet labeled "Stories": in the center circle is My story; in the next larger circle, Family and community stories; and in the largest circle, God's story. Referring to the largest circle, I usually mention the difference between limiting God's story to the Bible and including earth/cosmos as part of God's creation story.

Before you begin, write the journal question on newsprint that you will be asking people to think about, such as *"What story have I recently reclaimed in each circle?"* This will help you move toward the question with your story, and it will focus people's attention. You can also itemize on newsprint the main points you will be covering. For example:

- Masks & Mirrors
- Hero & Hearthkeeper
- Witness & Waiting

Take about 20 minutes for this input and be sure to include a personal story with some degree of vulnerability in it. Retreat participants can admire our skills and successes, but they will identify with our struggles.

9:35   Give people about 10 minutes to reflect in their journals on the focus question.

9:45   Give the Quads some time to share their reflections. Let them know how much time they have. You might suggest they appoint a timekeeper for the group in order to encourage self-monitoring and to give each person "equal air-time." For example, I might say, "Share whatever you want to say from your response to this stage with your Quad. Your group will have about 30 minutes for sharing. I will ring a chime at the end of this time, and then there will be a short break."

10:15   BREAK

10:30 A.M. to 12:00 P.M.
Stage Three: REVELATION

10:30   A third leadership team member should introduce this segment of the soulwork cycle, using the same format as above. Take about 20 minutes to focus on the idea of call. This may be a new idea for people, so you will need to include material from the first chapter on CALL as well as the chapter on REVELATION. Include a story from your own life that illustrates an experience you have had of REVELATION. The story you tell will provide a model for participants, giving them clues about how deep and how personal they can be in their sharing.

10:50   Allowing about 25 minutes for journal time, ask participants to make a timeline of their lives, then divide it into "chapters" and give a title to each chapter. Ask them to focus on the chapters from the standpoint of call or guidance and make a few notes about their experience of REVELATION.

11:15   Give Quads about 45 minutes for sharing from their timelines.

12:00 to 3:00
LUNCH & FREE TIME
Before lunch, remind people that the schedule provides for free time between lunch and 3:00 o'clock. Encourage people to walk

or rest, recall parts of the morning that seemed troubling or particularly appealing, and be ready to meet for an extended sharing session when they come back at 3:00.

3:00 to 5:30 P.M.
POISON RIVER and Stage Four: RISK

3:00   A selected team member should offer a framework for extended sharing by presenting input on the shift from private spirituality to public action from the POISON RIVER chapter. If you can use your own timeline "chapters" as an example, it will help participants see that they are already involved in the RISK stage by sharing what is important to them with others at the retreat. You can broaden the focus of your input here to include the POISON RIVER as a place of indecision and hesitation, possibly anger and regret, and maybe add a section to your timeline that looks toward the future. Model a personal story about a RISK you have recently taken that will have an impact on your future.

3:30   At this point in the design, give the Quads about 2 hours together, so each person will have about 15 minutes to tell her story of call in some detail and another 10 minutes or so for some "mirroring" from the group. I usually remind the Quads to choose a timekeeper and take a stretch break between speakers. Quads might want to move to another room for this extended time of sharing. The group as a whole will not meet again until after dinner.

5:30 - 7:00 P.M.
DINNER & FREE TIME

7:00 to 10:00 P.M.
Stage Five: RELATE

7:00   When you gather after dinner, take about half an hour to sing and maybe do some simple stretching together. This is an important time of regrouping with the whole community after the intensive Quad time in the afternoon.

7:30   A selected team member should give some input from the RELATE chapter, emphasizing the importance of finding a new community to support a new call. Begin by retelling the Gideon and Esther story, noting that the RELATE stage is where call is made visible. This is a good spot to point out the polarity between RECLAIM and RELATE, as well as the polarity between RESIST and RISK. The personal story that you provide in this input should describe a community that is important to you . . . and why.

At this point I like to introduce some kind of nonverbal activity that will help people integrate what they are discovering. It could be art or drama or movement or meditation or . . . The point is for each person to make images or metaphors from their own experience. One possibility is to have each leadership team member to be in charge of a different activity (poetry, clay, banner-making, or a modern dramatization of Gideon or Esther). Give people about an hour for this project

8:30   Come back together for a time of sharing these "projects" with the whole group.

End the evening in a candlelit circle around the informal altar. Allow for some quiet sharing and prayer time. There is real power in a gathered community that has, by now, been through a soul journey together. Do not try to structure the sharing too much. I have found that ending this way gives the introverts permission to go off to bed quietly and the extroverts time to stay and visit in the main room.

• *SUNDAY* •

Again provide a quiet place for people to have a sitting meditation together before breakfast if they want it.

9:00 to 10:30 A.M.
Stage Six: RELEASE

9:00 Begin with stretching and singing to help gather the whole group for the final session.

9:15 A selected team member should provide input from the RELEASE chapter. This input might begin with how people hate to say "good-bye." Input from the stories of Esther and Gideon can point out the importance of seeing one's story in a larger sweep of history because that gives us a sense of meaning and purpose in endings as a preparation for new beginnings.

I like to revisit the entire soulwork cycle at this point, making connections between what the group has done together and each stage of the cycle. It is a way to empower people to use the material personally and in groups. I usually pick an image from Gideon or Esther on which to focus—either the golden loincloth that became a snare to Gideon and his family, or the two dragons and Esther as the river between—as a reminder that nobody does it perfectly, even biblical heroes!

9:45 Allow about 15 minutes of journaling time for people to respond to these questions:

- *What is my next step in claiming my call?*
- *What barriers or blocks can I expect?*
- *What resources do I have for moving past them?*

10:00 Give Quads 30 minutes to share from their journal responses and affirm the gifts they have been to each other.

10:30 BREAK

10:45 A.M. to 12:00 P.M.
WORSHIP

10:45   Close with an informal worship in the same space where you have been meeting, to suggest our power to make a place holy with the sacredness of our lives. Give people time to share their special gifts with the whole community. I like to include these elements:

- An invitation to gather.
- A song that has become important to the group.
- A prayer to honor God's gift of community
- Any poems, readings, or other offerings.
- Sharing "What I have received from this retreat."
- A closing song and word from the leader to send us forth into the world.

• *ONE-DAY DESIGN* •
9:00 A.M. to 4:00 P.M.

If I were going to present the soulwork cycle in a shorter format, I would do it with one other team member to streamline the upfront leadership. You can follow the basic retreat design I have outlined on the preceding pages, making the following modifications to fit your one-day structure.

9:00   Make name tags and have coffee/tea available as people come in.

9:15 - 10:15
    Do not be tempted to shortchange the necessity for establishing a *safe* environment. Allow people to name themselves into the circle and do some "mixers" in order to get a feel for the group. Have people form groups of 3 (which will take less time for sharing than groups of 4).

10:15 - 11:00

Stage One: RESIST
Following the retreat design, allow for a 15-minute input, 10 minutes of journaling, and 15 minutes of sharing in Triads, followed by a short break.

11:00 -11:45

Stage Two: RECLAIM
Allow for a 15-minute input, 10 minutes of journaling, and 15 minutes of sharing in Triads. Creating a timeline is still an important exercise, but people will have less time to share from their journaling than they would have on a full weekend. Doing the timeline will give them something to work with later.

11:45 - 1:30

Stage Three: REVELATION
Introduce the theme of REVELATION and art materials that will be available during the lunch period. Suggest that people make an image of their call as they see it right now. Both team members should be present with the art materials to offer help and encouragement as people come to the "activity center."

1:30 - 2:30

POISON RIVER and Stage Four: RISK
Give an input on POISON RIVER followed by RISK. Ask people to take a RISK by sharing with their Triad the image they have made.

2:30   BREAK

2:45 - 3:30

Stage Five: RELATE and Stage Six: RELEASE
Give inputs for the last two stages, followed by a final time with Triads.

3:30 - 4:00

Come together for a closing worship and sharing.

Notes

The Nature of Call

1. Sam Shoemaker, "What Shall Religion Emphasize Today?" *The Calvary Evangel* (March 1927), 9.
2. Gordon Cosby, *By Grace Transformed*, 148.
3. William Bridges, "Getting Them Through the Wilderness: A Leader's Guide to Transition," unpublished training material.

The Cycle of Call

1. Gideon's story is found in the Book of Judges, chapters 6-8. All Gideon quotes come from the *New Revised Standard Version* (NRSV) translation of the Bible.
2. Esther's story is the whole Book of Esther from the Hebrew Testament of the Bible. Quotes in Esther come from *The Jerusalem Bible* (JB).

Stage One: Resist

1. Elizabeth O'Connor, *Cry Pain, Cry Hope*, 17.
2. O'Connor, Ibid., 35.
3. Personal communication.
4. Carol Pearson, *Awakening the Heroes Within*, Innocent, 79 and Orphan, 90.
5. Madonna Kolbenschlag, *Lost in the Land of Oz*, 163.
6. Elizabeth O'Connor, "What the World Needs Is Saints," *Faith@Work Magazine* (October 1963).

Stage Two: Reclaim

1. James Hillman, *The Soul's Code*, 7.
2. Alice Miller, *The Drama of the Gifted Child*, 14.
3. Elizabeth O'Connor, *The Eighth Day of Creation*.
4. Marjory Bankson, "The Craft of Creativity," *Grace* (Jan-Feb 1999), 10.
5. Joseph Campbell, *Hero with a Thousand Faces*, 30.
6. Sandra Wooten, *Touching the Body, Reaching the Soul*, 23.
7. Radio interview with Coretta Scott King, January 15, 1988, National Public Radio.
8. Matthew 22:37-40, NRSV.
9. Walter Wink, *The Powers That Be*, 18.
10. Roberta Hestenes, "In God's Image," in Moyers, *Genesis*, 30.

Stage Three: Revelation

1. Gordon Cosby, *By Grace Transformed*, 115ff.
2. Joseph Campbell, *Hero with a Thousand Faces*, 151.
3. Carol Pearson, *Awakening the Heroes Within*, Lover, 157 and Seeker, 132.
4. John Sanford, *The Invisible Partners*, 19.
5. Robert Greenleaf, *Servant Leadership*, 8.
6. Carolyn Shields, unpublished letter, March 1997.

The Poison River

1. Leonard Biallas, *Myths: Gods, Heroes, and Saviors*, 97.
2. M.C. Richards, conversation at Camp Hill Village, PA, September 1998.
3. Hermann Hesse, *Siddhartha*, 121.
4. Temptations of Jesus, Luke 4:1-13.
5. David Lloyd, "Preparing the Way of the Lord," unpublished sermon, December 7, 1997.

Stage Four: Risk

1. Anne Beaufort, unpublished journal entry, March 1998.
2. Margaret Wheatley, "What Is Our Work?," in Larry C. Spears (ed), *Insights on Leadership*, 346.
3. Gordon Cosby, *By Grace Transformed*, 27.
4. Margreta Silverstone, "Wilderness," unpublished sermon, March 15, 1998.
5. Leonard Biallas, *Myths: Gods, Heroes, and Saviors*, 180.
6. Jean Shinoda Bolen, *Goddesses in Every Woman*, 75ff.
7. Kate Amoss, "Sea Purple and Saffron: Gifting the Goddess: An Inquiry into Weaving, Healing and Athena's New Clothes," unpublished thesis, March 6, 1998.

Stage Five: Relate

1. Richard Heckler, *Holding the Center*, 65.
2. Margaret Wheatley, "What Is Our Work?," in Larry C. Spears (ed), *Insights on Leadership*, 349.
3. Joseph Campbell, *Hero with a Thousand Faces*, 193ff.
4. Robert Moore and Douglas Gillette, *King, Warrior, Magician, Lover*, 58.
5. Moore and Gillette, Ibid, 106.
6. Marcus Borg, *Meeting Jesus Again for the First Time*, 128.

7. Peter Bankson, "Finding My Way in the Wilderness," unpublished sermon, March 22, 1998.

8. Jesse Palidofsky, spiritual report to the author, March 1997.

Stage Six: Release

1. The description of the Sage and Fool archetypes comes from Ann and Barry Ulanov's *The Witch and the Clown*, 76 and 185ff. However, I have used the names "Sage" and "Fool," which are Carol Pearson's names for these archetypes.

2. I Corinthians 1:25, NRSV.

3. An excerpt of this Greenleaf essay can be found in Larry C. Spears (ed), *Insights on Leadership*, 15ff.

4. From the Table of Contents in Larry C. Spears (ed), *Insights on Leadership*.

5. Erik Erikson, *The Life Cycle Completed*, 32.

6. Ron Arms, "A Good Enough Commitment," unpublished sermon, September 20, 1998.

7. Donna Schaper, *Sabbath Sense*, 15.

8. Elizabeth O'Connor, *Wellspring* newsletter, September 1996. Elizabeth O'Connor died October 17, 1998.

Headwaters

1. Stanley Hauerwas and Will Willimon, *Resident Aliens*, 16.

Bibliography

Arms, Ron. Sermon. "A Good Enough Commitment," Unpublished sermon. September 20, 1998. (Available at www.seekerschurch.org)

Bankson, Marjory. "Death as a Passage." *Faith@Work Magazine*. Winter 1998. (Available at www.faithatwork.com)

Bankson, Marjory. "The Craft of Creativity." *Grace: A Companion for Women on their Spiritual Journey*. Jan-Feb 1999.

Bankson, Peter. "Finding My Way in the Wilderness." Unpublished sermon. March 22, 1998. (Available at www.seekerschurch.org)

Biallas, Leonard. *Myths: Gods, Heroes, and Saviors*. Mystic, CT: Twenty-Third Publications, 1986.

Bolen, Jean Shinoda. *Goddesses in Every Woman*. New York: Harper Colophon Books, 1984.

Borg, Marcus. *Meeting Jesus Again for the First Time*. San Francisco: HarperSanFrancisco, 1995.

Bridges, William. *Transitions*. Reading, MA: Perseus Books, 1980.

Brock, Lillie, and Mary Ann Solerno. *The InterChange Cycle*. Washington, D.C.: Bridgebuilder Media, 1994. (www. changecycle.com)

Campbell, Joseph. *Hero With a Thousand Faces*. Princeton University Press, Bollingen Series XVII, 1973.

Cosby, Gordon. *By Grace Transformed*. New York: Crossroad Publishing Co, 1999.

Crum, Thomas. *Journey to Center: Lessons in Unifying Body, Mind and Spirit*. New York: Simon & Schuster, 1997.

Edinger, Edward. *Ego and Archetype*. Boston: Shambhala, 1992.

Erikson, Erik. *The Life Cycle Completed*. New York: W.W. Norton, 1982.

Estes, Clarissa Pinkola. *Women Who Run With The Wolves: Myths and Stories of the Wild Woman Archetype*. New York: Ballantine Books, 1992.

Greenleaf, Robert. *On Becoming a Servant Leader*. San Francisco: Jossey-Bass, 1996.

___. *The Power of Servant Leadership*. San Francisco: Berrett-Koehler Publishers, 1998.

___. *The Servant Leader*. Peterborough, NH: Windy Row Press, 1970.

___. *Servant Leadership*. Mahwah, NJ: Paulist Press, 1983.

___. "The Servant as Leader." In *Insights on Leadership* (Larry C. Spears, Ed.). New York: John Wiley & Sons, 1998.

Hahn, Thich Nhat. *Living Buddha, Living Christ.* New York: Riverhead Books (G. P. Putnam's Sons), 1995.

Hauerwas, Stanley, and William H. Willimon. *Resident Aliens.* Nashville: Abingdon Press, 1989.

Heckler, Richard Strozzi. *Holding the Center.* Berkeley, CA: Frog, Ltd., 1997.

Hendricks, Harville. *Getting the Love You Want.* New York: Henry Holt & Co.,1988.

Hesse, Herman. *Siddhartha.* New York: New Directions. 1951.

Hillman, James. *The Soul's Code: In Search of Character and Calling.* New York: Random House, 1996.

Kolbenschlag, Madonna. *Lost in the Land of Oz: Befriending Your Inner Orphan and Heading for Home.* New York: Crossroad, 1994.

Levoy, Gregg. *Callings: Finding and Following an Authentic Life.* New York: Harmony Books, 1997.

Lloyd, David. Sermon. "Preparing the Way of the Lord." Unpublished sermon. December 7, 1997. (Available at www.seekerschurch.org)

May, Rollo. *The Cry for Myth.* New York: Dell (Bantam, Doubleday), 1991.

Miller, Alice. *The Drama of the Gifted Child.* New York: Basic Books, 1981.

Moody, Harry R., and David L. Carroll. *The Five Stages of the Soul.* New York: Anchor Books, 1997.

Moore, Robert, and Douglas Gillette. *King, Warrior, Magician, Lover.* San Francisco: HarperCollins, 1990.

Moyers, Bill. *Genesis: A Living Conversation.* New York: Doubleday, 1996.

Nouwen, Henri J. M. *In the Name of Jesus.* New York: Crossroad, 1989.

___. *Life of the Beloved: Spiritual Living in a Secular World.* New York: Crossroad, 1994.

___. *Sabbatical Journey: The Diary of His Final Year.* New York: Crossroad, 1998

O'Connor, Elizabeth. *Cry Pain, Cry Hope: Thresholds to Purpose.* Waco, TX: Word Books, 1987.

___. *The Eighth Day of Creation.* Waco, TX: Work Books, 1971.

O'Connor, Elizabeth. "What the World Needs Is Saints." *Faith@Work Magazine.* October 1963. (Available at www.faithatwork.com)

Pearson, Carol. *Awakening the Heroes Within.* San Francisco: HarperCollins, 1991.

Richards, Mary Caroline. *Centering in Pottery, Poetry, and the Person.* Middletown, CT: Wesleyan University Press. 1962 and 1989.

___. *Imagine Inventing Yellow*. Barrytown NY: Station Hill. 1991.

Roof, Wade Clark. *A Generation of Seekers: The Spiritual Journeys of the Baby Boom Generation*. San Francisco: HarperCollins, 1993.

Sanford, John. *The Invisible Partners*. Mahwah, NJ: Paulist Press, 1984.

Schaper, Donna. *Sabbath Sense: A Spiritual Antidote for the Overworked*. Philadelphia: Innisfree Press, 1997

Shoemaker, Sam. "What Shall Religion Emphasize Today?" *The Calvary Evangel*. March 1927. (Available through Faith At Work, 106 E. Broad St., Ste B, Falls Church, VA 22046-4501.)

Silverstone, Margreta. "Wilderness." Unpublished sermon. March 15, 1998. (Available at www.seekerschurch.org)

Spears, Larry C. (ed.) *Insights on Leadership*. New York: John Wiley & Sons, 1998.

Stein, Murray. *Jung's Map of the Soul*. Chicago: Open Court, 1998.

Swimme, Brian, and Thomas Berry. *The Universe Story*. San Francisco: HarperCollins, 1992.

Ulanov, Ann and Barry. *Religion and the Unconscious*. Philadelphia: Westminster Press, 1975.

___. *The Witch and the Clown: Two Archetypes of Human Sexuality*. Wilmette, OR: Chiron Publications, 1987.

Wheatley, Margaret. *Leadership and the New Science: Learning about Organization from an Orderly Universe*. San Francisco: Berrett-Koehler, 1994.

___. "What Is Our Work?" In *Insights on Leadership* (Larry C. Spears, ed.). New York: John Wiley & Sons, 1998

Wink, Walter. *The Powers That Be: Theology for a New Millennium*. New York: Doubleday, 1998.

Wooten, Sandra. *Touching the Body, Reaching the Soul*. Taos: Mountain Press, 1995.

OTHER RESOURCES FROM AUGSBURG

Seasons of Friendship by Marjory Zoet Bankson
160 pages, 0-8066-9016-X (current edition, available now)
0-8066-5136-9 (rev. edition, January 2005)

Traces the cycles of Naomi and Ruth for clues about women's needs for varying friendships in different seasons of life.

Your Call Is Waiting by Terry-Anne Preston
192 pages, 0-8066-4160-6

Follow the method outlined in *Your Call Is Waiting* to discern your own call within God's plan. Questions, charts, lists, and contemplation of biblical examples of calling will lead you to your answer. To enhance this process, the author includes a thirty-day Bible study that will focus your mind and spirit on your calling.

Listen! God Is Walling! by D. Michael Bennethum
96 pages, 0-8066-4991-7

God's call to faithful living is often understood primarily in terms of bein¡ involved in church-sponsored ministries. In *Listen! God Is Calling!* author D. Michael Bennethum presents Martin Luther's teaching on vocation as resource both for individual believers, helping them find deeper meaning in their ordinary daily labors; and for congregations, encouraging them t¡ develop a climate that supports their members at work.

Signs of Belonging by Mary E. Hinkle
96 pages, 0-8066-4997-6

Signs of Belonging: Luther's Marks of the Church and the Christian Life explores Luther's teaching on the seven marks of the church: possession of the Word, Baptism, Sacrament of the Altar, Office of the Keys, Office of Ministry, Discipleship, and the cross.

Available wherever books are sold.